Containing the Uncontainable

Alcohol Misuse and the Personal Choice Community Programme

BARBARA ELLIOTT BSc, CQSW, DipApSS
University of Bath

D1610222

W
WHURR PUBLISHERS
LONDON AND PHILADELPHIA

British Library Cataloguing in Publication Data

A catalogue record for this book
is available from the British Library.

ISBN 1 86156 368 X

Typeset by Adrian McLaughlin, a@microguides.net
Printed and bound in the UK by Athenæum Press Ltd, Gateshead,
Tyne & Wear.

Contents

Foreword

PHILIP J FLORES

This is a relatively short book that addresses an enormous problem in a very comprehensive way. Barbara Elliott has done a painstakingly objective blending of a number of diverse perspectives on the treatment of substance misuse and integrated them into a practical, yet theoretically sound model she calls the Personal Choice Community Programme (PCCP). In the book, she describes ways that PCCP incorporates a number (seven to be exact) of different interventions, all of which share a common ingredient proven to be helpful in the treatment of substance abuse.

The underlying theme these different interventions share is consistently simple. They reflect a fundamental, but profound fact: amongst substance abusers that opt for formal treatment, those that stay in treatment demonstrate the most improvement. Elliott quickly recognizes a sometimes overlooked, but crucial ingredient about substance abuse treatment: for many, successful addiction treatment is dose related. The more treatment provided and the longer treatment continues (up to an optimum amount), the better the outcome. She encourages treatment providers to examine the ways their treatment and program structure fails to carefully manage treatment retention. Consequently, all strategies need to be geared towards reducing dropouts.

Early in the book, Elliott quickly plunges into the important question that has plagued the addiction treatment field for years. Why do some substance abusers demonstrate a greater propensity to benefit from treatment while others do not respond as favorably? The question of whether certain kinds of clients may respond better to certain kinds of treatment has been most extensively investigated over the years, culminating recently in the massive and eagerly awaited Project MATCH Study (1998). Project MATCH tested three distinct interventions (Alcoholics Anonymous, cognitive behavioral, and motivational enhancement) and randomly assigned subjects to each group to determine if substance abusers would do better in treatment if their characteristics and needs were matched to particular, relevant interventions. The findings from the study were awaited with excitement and anticipation within the addiction treatment community. The results, indicating that neither approach was more successful than another, were stunning.

Drawing on the findings of the massive Match Study, Elliott astutely interprets the data to draw some important conclusions and recommendations. Her analysis of the results reveal that there are some very important inferences to be drawn from this work, if one searches below the surface of the study's initial conclusions. A consistent percentage (around 30 percent) of substance abusers opting for abstinence (defined as treatment-receptive clients) will respond positively to any form of treatment as long as adequately trained therapists who are skilled at establishing a working therapeutic alliance provide it. The rest (defined as treatment-resistant clients) are more likely to fail in their abstinence goal for mutually shared reasons related to patient characteristics in conjunction with program or therapist variables that fail to enhance treatment retention. Her insightful interpretations lead her to draw some impressive conclusions about the way a treatment program needs to be structured.

Elliott correctly makes the important suggestion that it would be more productive to focus on what it is that increases treatment retention, regardless of the orientation or treatment modality that is being employed. Evidence suggests that certain variables can contribute to dropouts, especially for the most vulnerable individuals. She identifies the major contributions to treatment dropouts as those variables–either therapist or program structure–that lead to ruptures in the treatment alliance. Disruptions can be caused by either the therapist's failures in properly managing the therapeutic alliance (i.e. empathic failures related to transference intensity, counter-dependent acting-out, projective identification, etc.) or because of transitions in the treatment program (i.e. transitions from primary care to aftercare, rotating therapists, holidays/illness interruptions to continuity of care, etc.) that are not carefully monitored. Interruptions or ruptures in the attachment or therapeutic alliance, she concludes, will obviously prove to be more difficult for treatment-resistant clients to tolerate.

Disruptions in the attachment alliance are always related to either therapist's failures or inadequate program structure and this book focuses on those program structure variables which can directly effect therapist variables. If one examines the common elements in all treatment outcome studies across the entire range of different disorders, it is evident that failures to establish or maintain the therapeutic alliance is the single most important contributor to treatment failure and treatment dropout, regardless of diagnostic categories. This is especially true for this popula-

tion because of the special circumstances (i.e. co-occurring Axis II disorder, cortical compromise secondary to substance induced encephalopa-
thy, acute crisis, chronic stress, etc.) that many substance abusers bring to
treatment. Treatment-resistant substance abusers are more likely to be
treatment failures because they don't remain in treatment due to ruptures
in the therapeutic alliance, and these ruptures are often related to anti-
quated models of treatment that fail to recognize the special demands
that many substance abusers bring to treatment. Approaches that typically work with the non-substance abuser will not work with this population.
These patients typically need more gratification, structure, and responsiveness if they are to be engaged and remain in treatment. Successful
engagement hinges on the managing and establishment of the therapeutic alliance, or what I will refer to as an attachment to treatment and
recovery. Besides the difficulties inherent in managing any therapeutic
relationship (it is just more difficult with substance abusers), Elliott's
work leads one to ask how can treatment retention be enhanced.

The PCCP model presented in this book continually addresses this
question and is built on the foundation of correcting this problem. Elliott
appropriately recognizes that the biggest obstacle to successful treatment
is the failure of treatment retention. If proper program structure and therapy strategies are implemented, treatment dropouts can be reduced.
Elliott further suggests that treatment-resistant patients are the ones most
vulnerable to disruptions in treatment. Whether these disruptions occur
because of transitions in care (i.e. from primary care to aftercare) or
because of therapist's failure to manage negative transference and
empathic ruptures, the problem remains the same. Substance abusers
have special difficulties establishing a working therapeutic alliance and
are extremely vulnerable to anything that may disrupt the attachment
relationship. Robust research findings suggest repeatedly that a positive
therapeutic alliance, which can be viewed as secure attachment, is the
best overall predictor of good outcome in all forms of psychotherapy. The
emphasis on the significance of the attachment bond is another way to
speak of the strength of the therapeutic alliance. As Elliott suggests,
nowhere is this truer than with the addicted patient; and nowhere is this
more difficult to maintain than with the substance-abusing individual.

Philip J Flores, PhD

Philip J Flores PhD is a clinical psychologist who has worked extensively for the past
twenty years in the area of addictive disorders and group psychotherapy. In addition
to his book, *Group Psychotherapy with Addictive Populations*, he has published
numerous articles and chapters on addiction and group psychotherapy. Dr Flores'
new book, *Addiction as an Attachment Disorder*, is published by Jason Aronson.

Preface

I was introduced to the substance misuse field by accident, having applied late to do social work training and then needing to arrange a last-minute work placement quickly. Although I dreaded the idea of working with 'alcoholics' I agreed to go to a voluntary sector,[1] abstinence-based day centre in London, which offered an eclectic, psychosocial day programme. I soon found myself transfixed by the client group and the innovative interventions and therapies on offer to them. The only thing that bothered me during the placement was that every week numbers of clients disappeared off the programme without warning. Looking over the client register of that past year, it appeared that leaving without notice was a regular pattern. It surprised me that those who were 'lost' were not often discussed much by the multi-disciplinary staff team in their weekly meetings. Once they were gone, they were gone, the assumption being that if they failed to respond to follow-up letters and offers of further help, then they were inadequately motivated. It was hoped that they might get in touch again at a later date.

During my 11 weeks I thought a lot about what might be causing the exodus. Most of the people who disappeared seemed to me highly motivated and engaged so I decided that the day programme must have had a few things wrong with it structurally. When I qualified as a social worker the following year, I looked for a job in the alcohol field where I could put some of my work placement experiences and fresh theories into practice.

I was delighted when I was offered a job as manager of a small day service in West London where a six-week 10:00 a.m. to 4:00 p.m. programme was already in operation, and I set to work implementing some changes in conjunction with the rest of the therapy team. Satisfied with the improvements I had brought to the programme, I then sat back and watched to see what would happen next. I was again struck by the optimism and high spirits of our recovering clients. It was very close to the atmosphere I had so enjoyed on my student placement. Unlike those in hospitals or residential units, I thought, our clients were free to choose. They had only to walk in the door, ask for help and they could begin the day programme within the week. Surely their optimism and willingness to work hard in therapy was due to the fact that they were truly motivated, had come out of choice and knew they were free to stop coming at any time. These individuals were there because they wanted to be. It was all extremely satisfying and I was sure that I had made the right choice in coming into the alcohol treatment field. Events would soon shatter these naive expectations.

Over the first six months, I witnessed many clients come to the day centre, join the day programme (which they were expected to attend daily for the full six weeks) and then unexpectedly relapse. Some clients relapsed in the early days of starting treatment. Others relapsed later, a few in their sixth and final week. Those who had completed six weeks were expected to come back on a weekly basis for follow-up counselling. To my amazement, even these champions who had completed the course rarely made it back for follow-up beyond three or six months and some not even beyond a few sessions. Not only did the majority of our clients relapse at some time during their treatment or follow-up but most of them never got in touch again. They had simply disappeared.

Throughout my first year in the day centre service, I became used to this pattern. My reaction and that of my colleagues was to become more entrenched in our practices and ideas about 'treatment'. We positively reinforced the many clients who expressed relief and gratitude at being 'off the booze' and in a programme that they liked and that they experienced as helpful. They seemed so sure, so clear, so strong. They truly understood that you couldn't stay stopped because of pressure or trouble, even if that was what had led to the original decision to get help. You could only really stop if you wanted to. Yet, many of these individuals, while seemingly engaged with the treatment process, inexplicably relapsed.

What was even more perplexing to me was the kind of interaction (or lack of it) going on between our local Alcoholics Anonymous/Twelve Step practitioners and the more psychoanalytically oriented clinicians I knew and worked with. In some cases there was actual mistrust and contempt, with increasing factionalization occurring between camps. While I became more and more demoralized, the staff team I managed, supervised and worked alongside seemed oblivious to the numbers of clients who were not achieving their stated aims. This is easy when there are many more needy individuals at the front door clambering to get in and start their physical and psychological recovery. In despair, I began to think that my generic psychotherapy colleagues were right after all. Substance misusers were just too difficult to treat. I considered moving out of the field altogether but instead began to think seriously about how we might change our approach to treatment.

The Personal Choice Community Programme (PCCP) is a response to these early experiences and has been developed over many years in different settings, with the single aim of increasing the odds for problem drinkers approaching abstinence-based services for help. In the United States, Alcoholics Anonymous/Twelve Step approaches are the most popular form of intervention for substance misusers. In the United Kingdom, Alcoholics Anonymous is less culturally acceptable although it too is growing in influence. The Personal Choice Community Programme is designed specifically for individuals who cannot make use of Alcoholics Anonymous, yet need an intensive, supportive, abstinence-based treatment experience. The technique described falls somewhere between psychodynamic models which, to my mind, are often too analytic in practice, and cognitive behavioural models, which do not tend to take much account of unconscious experience. Consequently, I believe it is the first structural integration of the two approaches in an alcohol treatment programme. The model should be of interest to professionals in the substance misuse field who have found that the psychosocial or cognitive behavioural programmes they operate are not particularly effective but who do not want to follow a strict Alcoholics Anonymous/Twelve Step approach. While the book describes a programme designed for alcohol misusers, the model has direct applications for the treatment of a wide range of substance misuse and can be easily adapted. It also has particular applications to work with eating disorders and a range of personality disorders. In fact, the model has applications to almost any of the so-called 'difficult-to-treat' groups, assuming that ongoing therapeutic work is desirable for the individuals concerned and that they are capable of settling into and travelling to a non-residential setting on a regular basis.

The ideas in this book should not be alien to generic psychodynamic counsellors, psychotherapists and group analytic therapists even if the treatment setting described is. I do hope, however, that a convincing case has been made for keeping most substance misusers away from the analytic consulting room. It is my belief that for the first two years following abstinence, the majority of substance misusers should be treated together in groups and not in generic individual or group therapy settings. After that, all being well, individuals needing or wanting further help should be good candidates for the wide range of non-specialist cognitive, behavioural and analytic psychotherapies on offer in the private and public sectors.

Barbara Elliott

[1] Voluntary sector services are traditionally registered charities that are run by management committees. They employ staff in the same way as the statutory sector and are usually funded by both government and charities.

Acknowledgements

If it is true that we only really learn from our mistakes (Bion 1962), then I have many, many former clients and patients to thank for what I know. My thanks also to Doug Cameron, the late Nina Coltart, Nina Farhi, Meg Sharpe and Betsy Thom who read and commented on an early paper which formed the basis of this book. I am grateful to Andrew Clark, Philip Flores, Earl Hopper, Michael Robinson, Paul Watts and Robert Young who read and commented on the manuscript and particularly to Edward Khantzian and Richard Velleman for their thoughtful and detailed responses. My thanks also to The Alcohol Education and Research Council who have funded a much appreciated research studentship which has enabled me to pursue related research at the University of Bath. I am indebted to the members of the Avon and Wiltshire Mental Health Partnership NHS Trust, Research and Development Unit who were endlessly supportive over the last 18 months of this book's preparation and particularly to Imogen Howse for her technical expertise, which enabled me to deliver a neat and tidy manuscript to my publisher. Lastly, I am thankful, grateful and indebted to David Elliott, without whom this book would not have been written.

It is also well known that after a few months infants of either sex become fond of playing with dolls, and that most mothers allow their infants some special object and expect them to become, as it were, addicted to such objects.

DW Winnicott, *Transitional Objects and Transitional Phenomena*,
1971: 1

... repeated experience with an appetitive activity can produce changes that increase the attraction that activity holds for a person. This increased attachment, which is best thought of as a 'strong appetite', has at least three components: affective attachment to the object of the appetite, behavioural intention to consume or approach that object, and cognitive commitment to the object and its approach or consumption.

Jim Orford, *Excessive Appetites: A Psychological View of Addictions*,
1985: 207

CHAPTER 1
Introduction

This book has been written for clinicians interested in developing new and more effective ways of working with certain kinds of problem drinkers. It can be read in its own right but has been designed particularly as a reference manual for those wishing to establish and then practise the PCCP model. For those who are not concerned with the underlying theory and influences on the model, a description of what the programme looks like and how it operates begins on page 44. Before moving on to influences and relevant theory however, the notion of a 'drinking problem' itself will be defined and explored.

There are several terms synonymous with problem drinking: chief among them are 'alcoholism', 'alcohol dependence' and 'alcohol misuse'. The term 'alcoholism', closely associated to the word 'addiction', refers to a state of chronic disease and is prominent in biomedical, including genetic, models of causation. In this book, a greater emphasis is placed on the psychosocial and/or cultural elements than on the physiological and therefore the term will not be used other than in contexts where it is the accepted language, e.g. in references to Alcoholics Anonymous. Alcohol (or substance) misuse is a term that refers to a difficulty in controlling consumption and continued consumption despite evidence of problems resulting from drinking. Alcohol misuse always involves a problematic use of alcohol but, as is the case with someone who engages in irregular binge drinking, does not necessarily involve a chronic use. Alcohol dependence refers to an ongoing compulsion to drink regardless of impairments to health or relationships. The dependence syndrome (Edwards and Gross 1976) includes features such as tolerance (the need for increasingly greater amounts in order to achieve the same effect), withdrawal symptoms (degrees of discomfort when stopping or cutting down), unsuccessful attempts to cut down, and increasingly more time spent in obtaining and using substances. While misuse can take place without any evidence of dependence, the two very often go hand in hand and both terms will be used in this book.

1

Just as there is no single term to describe the range of problem drinking, there is no such thing as a typical problem drinker. Alcohol problems know no age group, gender or class although recent trends suggest a worrying increase in consumption amongst Britain's women (Alcohol Concern 2002b) and the young, who often turn to alcohol as their drug of choice (DOH 2000, OPCS 1994). Despite a barrage of media coverage suggesting the contrary, the number of individuals dependent on alcohol is nearly twice that of those dependent on all illicit drugs put together (Alcohol Concern 1997). One in 25 of all adults in the UK fits the criteria for alcohol dependence (OPCS 1994) while 37 per cent of young men and 23 per cent of young women regularly (and dangerously) binge drink (ONS 2000).

In the United States, despite some fluctuations in overall levels of consumption, there are similar concerns, with 14 per cent of the population meeting the criteria for alcohol dependence at some time in their lives (Anthony et al. 1994)) and more than four times the loss of life than that associated with illicit drugs (USDHHS 2000). As is the case in the UK, alcohol is the number one drug of choice for teenagers, with 25 per cent of America's alcohol being consumed by the under-21s (CASA 2002). An estimated 20 per cent of 12–20-year-olds engage in regular binge drinking, with 16 per cent reporting blackouts following heavy drinking sessions (NIAAA 1998b). Girls in particular are beginning to drink at younger ages, with the numbers of 10–14-year-olds consuming alcohol rising from 7 per cent in the 1960s to a staggering 31 per cent in the 1990s (NHSDA 1996). Those who begin drinking before the age of 21 are twice as likely to develop alcohol-related problems and those starting before the age of 15 are four times more likely to become dependent on alcohol. These figures represent problems in later life where women problem drinkers are 40 per cent more likely to attempt suicide and 57 per cent more likely to become victims of violence than non-problem drinkers (NHSDA 1996). (For those interested in more information about the connection between alcohol, ill health and crime, details can be found in Appendix A.)

With alcohol misuse all around us, just how difficult is it to determine whether or not an individual has a genuine problem? The first step is usually to get a measure of an individual's regular weekly consumption by asking them to compile a drink diary. Recommended safe levels of consumption are generally accepted to be 14–21 units a week for women and 21–28 units a week for men spread over five to six days. There also exist a number of diagnostic tools, both brief (CAGE: Mayfield et al. 1974; MAST: Selzer 1971), and more lengthy (DSM-IV: American Psychiatric Association 1994; Alcohol Dependence Syndrome Checklist: Edwards and Gross 1976), which can help to identify dependence on alcohol. In the end, many practitioners prefer to rely on a simple four-factor criterion as their main diagnostic assessment tool. They look for any evidence that an individual's drinking is creating problems in these four areas:

1. their physical/psychological health, such as liver disease or depression
2. their family life or social relationships, such as arguments about excessive drinking
3. their work, such as warnings about taking long drinking lunches
4. their relationship with the law, such as drink-driving convictions.

Anyone who has not responded to problems in these areas by automatically reducing drinking patterns and rates of consumption is likely to have some kind of drinking problem. In the end, defining what does and what does not constitute a problem is a complex issue. Dependence should not so much be defined by how much an individual drinks as by how alcohol is used and the effects it has on drinkers and those around them (Edwards 2000).

Anyone with experience in the alcohol field will know that just as there is no such thing as a typical 'problem drinker', there is no such thing as a standard response to a drinking problem. For example, an individual may be regularly drinking at what are agreed to be harmful levels yet experience no problems for self or others. The same individual, on the other hand, may perceive his or her drinking to be problematic in some way, risking for example the loss of a job or a partner or good health, and may simply decide to stop, and do so successfully. He or she may stop following one or two chats with the family doctor about the risks to health (a brief intervention) or following between three and twelve sessions with a local alcohol counsellor (a lengthier brief intervention). This same individual may stop drinking following a spell in a group-based residential or day care programme or after attending Alcoholics Anonymous. He or she might stop, then return to harmful levels of consumption following attendance at a recovery programme, and then stop again later. Or the same individual might be exposed to any of these interventions and consequently bring alcohol consumption down to what would be viewed as a safe, controlled level and keep it there.

These scenarios are all examples of what could be considered serious drinking problems and their solutions. The treatment approach described in this handbook can be used as a response to this range of drinking problems; however, it has been designed especially for another group that does not fit into any of these categories. These are individuals who approach health services or support organizations because they know they are damaging some aspect of their lives through uncontrolled drinking and they have decided – usually following many failed attempts at control – to abstain from alcohol. They may also have support from family or friends, and be motivated to do something about their alcohol problem but, unlike any of the categories already described, these individuals fail either to control reasonably or abstain, no matter how many times they are offered help. These are the individuals who are often referred to as 'treatment-resistant' or 'revolving door' clients and constitute the group that has inspired the PCCP treatment model. The model itself is suitable only for those electing to abstain from alcohol; however, elements of the programme allow for an ongoing evaluation of the desirability of an abstinence goal when control might be a better or more realistic alternative. The programme itself is designed to operate specifically within a day centre or outpatient setting. Although the model was originally developed in response to the needs of problem drinkers, it has direct applications for the treatment of a wide range of drug users as well as for those with eating disorders or those diagnosed with personality disorders, and can be easily adapted.

Before examining the underlying theory of the model, some general assumptions about substance use and misuse are outlined in the following chapter. These themes should be incorporated into any staff training for those intending to practise the PCCP model. An informed, non-judgemental attitude to the use of drugs contributes to the creation of an underlying therapeutic culture where respect for individual personal choice is paramount.

CHAPTER 2

How do we define substance misuse?

Most societies condone the use of certain drugs and show a clear preference for particular types – alcohol or opiates, stimulants or depressants.
Misuse of substances may raise difficult moral and ethical questions and
arouse powerful feelings, both in the user and in those who witness such
use. Whether drug users are viewed as criminals or heroes and whether
they are offered help and support or incarceration and punishment is
based more often on economic and cultural constraints than on any
rational assessment of the intrinsic dangers of a particular substance.
Anthropological observations (e.g. Douglas 1987) of drug-taking behaviour from around the world suggest that the substances themselves are
not necessarily harmful. Even instances of extreme intoxication and dis-
inhibition, when organized within a cohesive, political/hierarchical
structure, can strengthen personal bonds, stabilize social/economic networks and promote healing through a resolution of unconscious conflict
(Bott 1987). Deviance and disturbance seem to arise in cultures where
drug-taking (including drinking) is encouraged and condoned, but where
such activity is divorced from strong, containing, multi-generational, hierarchical networks such as family structures or others. While, in most
cases, we cannot blame the harm associated with substance misuse on the
substances themselves, it seems apparent that problematic substance misuse is on the increase and is becoming a dominant, disruptive and
disturbing feature of modern life.

Within the United Kingdom, workers in voluntary, statutory and
health/social care sectors are seeing an ever-larger proportion of the population, who, having become dependent on some substance or a
combination of substances, are seeking help for their problems. It is
important to remain sensitive to the differences between various substances and, accordingly, to the differences between groups of individuals
who show a preference for one particular drug over another. At the same
time, there is far more that unifies users of legal and illicit drugs than that
which separates them (Orford 1985). Most problem drinkers are surprised

to learn about the medical consensus, which suggests that alcohol is inherently more damaging than many other drugs such as cannabis or heroin. Alcohol misusers may choose to disassociate themselves from other kinds of drug misusers (and vice versa). However, it is imperative that clinicians remain sensitive to the cultural, political and social determinants of concepts such as risk and harm across the range of substances, and then to integrate this understanding into their day-to-day exchanges with clients.

One issue about which clinicians wishing to practise the PCCP model must be informed concerns the long-standing debate regarding controlled drinking and drug use and practices relating to this. We know that, for example, many opiate users have no wish to abstain. Many experts in the illicit drug field have come to the conclusion that the safe, controlled use of drugs (such as heroin or methadone) is much better than the chaotic and unsafe use so characteristic of the illicit drug scene. A consequence of this view is that more drop-in and treatment centres, throughout the country, now seek to stabilize their clients, advising them on procedures for registering and drawing prescriptions and educating those clients about safe use. It is clear that for many people who abuse alcohol the option to control or limit harm is the more desirable choice and should always be on offer among a range of intervention options. Some individuals are able to control their intake to within safe limits and have no need even to consider abstinence. Others who drink harmfully will do better in the long run by focusing on reducing risk rather than by trying to stop altogether.

The debate over controlled drinking versus abstinence for those with a long-standing drink problem is far from resolved. Many abstinence-based programmes suffer from high drop-out rates and relatively poor long-term outcomes, but this does not necessarily mean that controlled drinking programmes are the answer or will do any better by their clients. For some individuals with an overwhelming desire for the effects of intoxication, it may be easier to try to live without any alcohol at all rather than with a little. The PCCP model is designed for those who have decided to abstain because they feel it will be easier for them to maintain abstinence over time. For the remainder who wish to try controlled drinking, solution-focused (Berg and Miller 1992) and cognitive behavioural techniques (Miller et al. 1991) offered within a counselling setting are an ideal place to start and can be easily accommodated within the same setting as an abstinence-based day service. This facilitates easy access from one type of intervention to the other for individuals who change their minds and change their goals over time.

CHAPTER 3

How does the PCCP model compare to other interventions?

A critique of seven common alcohol interventions and settings

Although the PCCP model is a new approach incorporating new techniques, it borrows elements from many existing models and practices. It is important, therefore, for the clinician to have a working understanding of those elements viewed as therapeutic (integrated into the model) and those viewed as problematic (excluded from the model) within each of the most common interventions and settings to be found in the United Kingdom today. For quick reference, a brief summary of the therapeutic and problematic elements will follow at the end of each section.

Alcoholics Anonymous

The best-known and most widely available form of help for people with drinking problems (3,426 groups in Britain, 50,997 in the USA) is Alcoholics Anonymous (AA). Alcoholics Anonymous was established in the United States in the 1930s, created by two alcoholics who managed to recover after years of compulsive, uncontrollable and destructive drinking. At the heart of their recovery programme was the notion that it takes an alcoholic to know an alcoholic, it takes an alcoholic to help an alcoholic, and it helps an alcoholic to help an alcoholic. These three convictions typify AA's approach to the treatment of the problem. Since its modest beginnings, Alcoholics Anonymous has developed into a vast, worldwide, organizational network. The point of direct contact for the alcoholic seeking help is the local AA meeting. Following the same pattern each time, meetings are highly structured, rather ceremonial events which provide hope, guidance and a close-knit, intimate setting as a replacement for the ritual and engagement often found in a drinking

7

environment. Meetings begin and end with traditional prayers or readings of wisdom and lessons from *The Big Book* and then are centred around the telling of a life story. A member of the group candidly details his or her decline through alcohol abuse and re-emergence as an individual with dignity and self-knowledge gained through the involvement with AA practice and principles. AA literature sets out a philosophy of life and, in carefully graded stages, seeks to lead the sufferer to recovery from the ravages of alcohol addiction. Following the programme involves careful study and a working through of 12 steps and traditions while new belief systems and behaviour patterns are gradually substituted for old ones. The final stage of the programme (Twelve Stepping) involves a recovering alcoholic offering guidance and support to another less recovered. This helps create the circular, ongoing nature of the AA experience – embracing the membership of a lifelong fellowship.

AA is both simple and sophisticated (Flores 1997). Through its structured meeting format and social networks, it establishes a strong subculture which enables even new members to form a clear sense of identity distinct from their drinking environments. Within the boundary of each AA meeting, an intense, intimate group experience framed by highly ritualized procedures draws members in and provides an excellent container for the dependency feelings which inevitably flare up during withdrawal and the early stages of recovery.

Many of the seemingly simple steps and sayings are deceptively complex in content and directly address some of the most problematic aspects of addiction psychopathology. For example, the First and Third Steps of Alcoholics Anonymous:

Step 1: We admitted we were powerless over alcohol – that our lives had become unmanageable.
Step 3. We made a decision to turn our will and our lives over to the care of God – as we understand him.

(Alcoholics Anonymous 1939)

The acknowledgement of a permanent, all-pervasive allergy to alcohol and a powerlessness to resist the compulsion to drink puts the problem drinker into what appears to be an impossible situation. But as Bateson (1971) has pointed out, a double-bind dilemma needn't result in total defeat or in madness. It can produce a new solution to what has previously been an entrenched and closed behaviour system. In the case of Steps One and Three, for example, the solution involves abandoning concepts such as will-power, self-control and good character, and embracing the notion of a benign, healing power beyond the self.

This paradigm shift helps to directly counteract the feature psychoanalytically defined as narcissistic (the wish and belief that one can control impulses, relationships and events) which is such a major factor for many of those who suffer from substance misuse problems. As a result of absorbing and integrating these steps, AA members may gradually give up the conviction that they have the power to control events around them. Because depression and anger aroused by the individual's lack of control has most likely contributed to heavy drinking in the past, it is seen as a prerequisite to any lasting recovery that this major perceptual shift takes place. For many, this can be facilitated by exposing oneself to and then gradually internalizing the 'Steps' and 'Traditions' of AA.

There is much in AA that can provide the structure and the learning necessary for a recovery from alcohol misuse. However, there are many dependent drinkers who find aspects of the AA programme problematic. The notion of alcoholism as a lifelong allergy or disease is unattractive to many and deters some problem drinkers from taking advantage of what AA has to offer. A dislike of the stigma associated with the disease model is not the same as a defensive denial of the seriousness of the problem, but the two are not easily distinguished within the AA philosophy.

The set pattern of meetings dictated by long-established tradition, though intended to instil comfort, security and familiarity, can create more problems than it solves for some individuals. The repetition of sayings and readings around the central feature of a sometimes monotonous 'life story' monologue follows the same formula, meeting after meeting. Participants – particularly new ones – are likely to experience a range of difficult thoughts and/or emotions which cannot be articulated within the ritualized format until near the close of each meeting. This can result in participants being left with feelings of frustration, boredom or, even worse, isolation and disturbance following meetings.

Although Alcoholics Anonymous is not in itself a religion and is open to atheists and agnostics, the references to God and a higher power throughout the AA literature gives the meetings a religious feel. Recovery from 'alcoholism' within the AA programme seems to invite a psychological surrender and re-birth similar to that found in many radical forms of religious conversion. This feature particularly disturbs and deters many people – especially the young – from seeking an affiliation with AA.

Summary

Therapeutic elements

- Provides extended social/support network with clear identity distinct from drinking culture.
- Provides intimate group support through shared experiences.
- Provides container for dependency feelings, which helps to support vulnerable members psychologically.

- Provides guidance, traditions and teachings, which help to create beneficial cognitive/perceptual shifts in relation to self and others.
- Provides extensive network, which enables free movement between meetings if conflict or frustration is experienced in a particular setting.
- Enables members to access as little or as much contact as desired.

Problematic elements

- The notion of alcoholism as a lifelong disease often meets resistance from those who resent being told what their problem is.
- The rigidity of practices and procedures in meetings can lead to feelings of boredom, isolation and anger in the listener who is invited to respond only after the completion of the life story (monologue as opposed to dialogue).
- The use of spiritual/religious concepts and language such as handing over to a higher power, is viewed as a prerequisite to recovery but is particularly difficult for those with authority and control issues.

Twelve Step programmes

Twelve Step programmes are the most common form of treatment in the United States and are becoming increasingly widely available in the UK. They are almost exclusively offered in residential settings and usually combine the treatment of alcohol problems with that of other drug abuse as well as problems such as eating disorders. The model combines elements of education about substance misuse and human psychology with individual counselling, group therapy, family therapy, an emphasis on physical fitness, non-therapy activities and group living. As the name suggests, attendance at AA meetings is central to this model, as is specific instruction and guidance about AA's Twelve Step programme.

Individuals who require an in-patient intervention usually present for treatment in a vulnerable psychological and/or physiological state and, as is the case with most problem drinkers entering treatment, self-esteem and morale are low. It is not surprising that those who have damaged themselves and their loved ones, or their social and employment relationships, do respond positively to respite within a close, supportive environment. Here there are other people with whom to identify and learn from, caring doctors and counsellors to speak to, opportunities to gain physical fitness, knowledge about one's illness and step-by-step instructions about the means to a recovery. In addition, an insight-oriented, cathartic, psychotherapeutic experience based upon individual counselling and small intimate group work is usually experienced as both supportive and helpfully confrontative. A family therapy component appears to be a key factor for some in the recovery process and most people undergoing a Twelve Step programme will gain knowledge and personal insight from their experiences. A certain proportion of them will abstain from alcohol and reconstruct their physical, psychological and social lives. For many others, however, the model is problematic both during and after treatment.

Though there are a few publicly funded units offering treatment based on this method in the UK, most Twelve Step treatment programmes are private. They are, traditionally, luxurious and highly resourced and this makes them expensive: reserved for the minority with private health insurance, those able to pay thousands of pounds for an average six-week stay or those fortunate enough to receive public funding. Because, in most cases, the programmes are residential, and in all cases are of a set duration, certain complications can arise. The intense involvement of therapeutic community living can be enormously moving and helpful in the short run, but the inevitable separation from the group at the end of six or eight weeks and the re-adjustment to home and work life is not well negotiated by many clients. This can result in sudden, serious relapse despite preparing clients prior to leaving and making follow-up arrangements for them. Some Twelve Step programmes do operate in day centre settings, although this is comparatively rare in the UK. While problems associated with an abrupt physical break from the treatment centre do not arise, the same issues associated with the end of attendance in a highly structured full-time programme still result in a considerable rate of relapse following completion, and prior to after-care attendance becoming established

Finally, supporters of Twelve Step programmes openly acknowledge that the AA programme is central to the ongoing treatment plan. Whatever the benefits derived from the psychotherapeutic, educational and medical components of treatment, it is the willingness to become fully immersed in the AA fellowship which seems to be the critical variable following discharge. Many of those who are not able to identify with AA philosophy and practice are, therefore, likely to relapse.

Summary

Therapeutic elements

- Provides a close and supportive group environment.
- Provides medical assessment and emphasizes a return to physical fitness.
- Provides education, advice and supportive psychotherapy across a wide range of different interventions and techniques.

Problematic elements

- The intensity of cathartic psychotherapy experiences may be too painful and overwhelming to some individuals, triggering 'acting out' behaviours.
- The support and companionship inherent in group life comes to an abrupt end at the completion of full-time residential (or day) attendance, often leading to difficulty in adjusting from clinic life to home life or second stage treatment.
- The recovery process is directly related to clients' willingness to follow the AA programme during and following completion of their residential stay.

Residential projects and therapeutic communities

Residential services borrow many of their practices from the British Therapeutic Community movement. This philosophy and form of treatment was developed directly out of work with shell-shocked soldiers at the Northfields Hospital near Birmingham during World War II, when psychiatrists working in military neurosis units began treating patients not individually but as members of small community groups. Treatment centred around the exploration of all aspects of day-to-day life in small and large group therapy sessions, where the details and covert meanings of interactions could be articulated and regularly worked through. An inability to communicate and to engage in activity that was experienced as satisfying on the wards was taken as an indication of an individual's disturbance and the exploration of these difficulties was central to therapeutic community life.

Today, most residential programmes for those recovering from alcohol problems bear little resemblance to the purist therapeutic community practice originating in the 1940s. However, several original features can be identified. The notion of group living as both supportive and intrinsically therapeutic is crucial to all residential programmes. Treatment is conceived of as a combination of day-to-day living experiences – learning to cook, shop, clean and co-exist together – as well as a commitment to group meetings and the counselling process. Most residential programmes encourage and view a return to work as part of the recovery process, and most offer follow-up counselling or drop-in evenings to ex-residents.

There can be little doubt that for some problem drinkers, a stay of between six and twelve months in a residential project provides some hope of stability and recovery, especially for those who are homeless or who come from disruptive and unstable backgrounds. Living with a group of individuals who are all abstinent and committed to recovery can in itself be beneficial. Learning to work through uncomfortable feelings and conflict with others can be psychologically strengthening, and there are those who would argue that after six months in a well-functioning therapeutic community a client should be emotionally equipped with much that is necessary to survive in life. However, for many, there are problems inherent in a lengthy residential experience.

For funders, residential programmes are expensive – both the length of time of the average residential stay and the considerable cost of running a large house can be prohibitive. Many people do not wish to leave their homes, families, friends or jobs for periods of up to a year. Even those who stay the course, viewing residential projects as a safe haven away from problematic relationships and past drinking associations, have to leave the community one day. No matter how much planning and care goes into preparing residents for leaving and no matter how much follow-up counselling is arranged for them, many residents, including those who have done particularly well, do not make the transition back to the wider community. Whether caused by loneliness, fear, anxiety, or a sense of loss for the setting as a whole, many clients seriously relapse in the run-up to discharge or shortly after.

Summary

Therapeutic elements

- Provides a stable, dry environment for the homeless or for those who are unable to break contacts with drinking relatives and friends.
- Provides a supportive, close-knit community.
- Provides opportunities to learn new ways of relating well with others as well as opportunities to learn practical skills.

Problematic elements

- Many individuals do not wish to leave home, work, and social contacts for long periods.
- The transition back into the wider community (especially when living alone) is difficult to achieve despite preparation for leaving being incorporated into the programme. The problems inherent in separation are rarely managed successfully even with those individuals who stabilize, develop and thrive within the community setting.

Cognitive and behavioural models

Cognitive and behavioural techniques are practised within a range of treatment settings throughout the United Kingdom and are the most commonly delivered intervention in the individual counselling setting. The unifying philosophy behind the interventions is straightforward and simple: problem drinkers are viewed as rational adults who are capable of making optimal choices about their future behaviour based on accurate information and help in assessing best personal options. These are likely to change over time and with personal experience (Cameron 1995). Individuals are enabled to make changes following an exploration of how they think and how they behave as well as how they feel (see, among others, Beck et al. 1993; Hester and Miller 1989; Saunders and Allsop 1991).

Behavioural and cognitive models both offer a range of techniques that provide positive, rational approaches to drinking problems. Learning how to relax or how to be appropriately assertive, or learning how to manage triggers that might lead to relapse and to plan for dealing with them, are all fundamental components of a good treatment programme. It is not enough for clients to begin to feel better or stronger or more stable if they do not have the tools that will enable them to avoid the many traps and hazards that face them in their choice of abstinence. Within this framework, drinking is viewed as goal-directed where drinking problems develop as a result of skewed thinking and behaviour. By mapping out personal psychological patterns and corresponding behaviours, a person's inconsistencies and irrationalities can be pinpointed and adjusted. With the help of information, advice, support, the challenging of redundant beliefs and the development of certain skills, problem drinkers should be able to engage actively and respond to their self-defined problems with creative, custom-made solutions.

The theoretical perspective underpinning the behavioural model of treatment ensures that alcohol misuse is not viewed as a disease or illness but rather as a learned behaviour that has become problematic over time. Just as one has learned (through subtle social and emotional cues) to misuse alcohol, one can learn, with the help of particular techniques, to control or abstain from alcohol. These techniques include stress management, relaxation and social skills training. Cognitive interventions, particularly techniques such as motivational interviewing (Miller et al. 1991) or solution-focused therapy (Berg and Miller 1992), explore individuals' conflicts and ambivalence about their drinking and try to assist by helping them to formulate and then move towards self-defined goals. These kinds of approaches imply an alternative view to the notion of the problem drinker as a passive victim of a disease, dependent upon experts for treatment, or needing to form lifelong affiliations to particular programmes as the only means of achieving lasting stability. Behavioural techniques also emphasize the active involvement of clients who, having made choices, then learn how to behave differently in the face of impulses that have seemed both uncontrollable and unmanageable. The emphasis is on the view of problem drinkers as individuals who can gain self-control by engaging in specific practices. This in turn helps them to achieve and maintain their desired aim.

Behavioural and cognitive interventions are positive, rational approaches that clearly help many problem drinkers to resolve their difficulties by offering a range of skills and techniques that will be useful to them and will contribute to a greater sense of self-control and self-esteem. However, for many, these methods do not seem sufficient to facilitate lasting changes in behaviour.

While the most popular cognitive therapies, particularly motivational interviewing and solution-focused therapy, explore inevitable conflict and ambivalence about drinking, these interventions are not designed to register other, more deeply unconscious, and often destructive impulses and conflicts.[1] It is sometimes these very elements of emotional life that create unmanageable feelings which in turn disturb the individual's ability and desire to abstain or even to continue with a chosen intervention with a specific clinician. In particular, issues concerned with dependency, authority or a tendency to swing between idealization and denigration of self and others is not usually articulated or worked through in pure behavioural or cognitive approaches. The resultant frustration, anger or despair often leads to relapse in clients who had been benefiting from newly learned skills.

At the heart of behavioural and cognitive models is the belief that most people who voluntarily seek help for an alcohol problem should be able to recover if assisted by good education, advice, training and knowledge about personal motivation and beliefs. We know that many of them do not. Often during the course of treatment, clients' abilities to learn become disturbed and blocked, and techniques that should help them to abstain or control their drinking are not remembered or used appropriately and therefore are not in the end effective. Many people successfully complete behavioural/cognitive programmes, learn a great deal, and then return to previous patterns of damaging consumption.

Summary

Therapeutic elements

- Emphasizes each client's active participation in problem-solving.
- Breaks down the concept of alcohol dependence as a disease.
- Teaches techniques that can lead to improved self-esteem and self-control

---

[1] Cognitive analytic therapy (Ryle 1990) is one intervention that is geared toward a deeper exploration of unconscious life within a cognitive framework. Because it is traditionally offered within a 16-session counselling structure, many of the difficulties associated with counselling interventions as discussed below, are like to occur).

Problematic elements

• Lack of focus on those unconscious factors which block learning and can lead to relapse, i.e. resisting boundaries or authority, becoming unhelpfully dependent on or attached to a counsellor.
• No access to transference/countertransference[2] relationship as potential learning material.

Counselling services (psychodynamic, motivational and cognitive behavioural)

Individual counselling is a feature of almost every kind of alcohol treatment programme and can be found in both residential and day services. It has been highlighted in the present critique as an intervention in its own right because community-based counselling services operate throughout Britain and are usually the first point of contact for anyone seeking help. These private, voluntary and statutory services have been established to provide information, advice and counselling to a wide range of problem drinkers and their families and friends.

There is little doubt that speaking to someone who is warm, friendly and knowledgeable about alcohol problems will be helpful in many ways to a problem drinker. Individuals engaging in long-term alcohol misuse usually suffer from a multitude of social and emotional problems as well as medical ones, and an open-format counselling session is a good place to begin an exploration of these underlying problems (Velleman 1992). In an intimate and confidential setting, clients are free to explore their confused feelings, their relationship problems and the difficulties encountered in day-to-day life. Here they are encouraged to express what has previously been undisclosed or even blocked from consciousness. Many of the useful strategies and techniques already outlined in the critique on cognitive and behavioural interventions are also most effectively offered and practised in a one-to-one setting. Both motivational interviewing and solution-focused counselling are designed for and most often delivered in an individual rather than a group setting. Counselling seems an excellent choice for those who are too timid or inhibited to meet with

---

[2] Transference refers to the patient's emotional attitude toward the therapist in any analytic therapy, in particular when ideas, feelings and characteristics attributed to the therapist belong not to the therapist but to a significant other in the patient's past, e.g. mother or father. Countertransference refers to the therapist's emotional attitude to the patient. This attitude can be taken up as a tool with which to better understand the patient's unconscious attitudes and experiences. (All definitions taken from Rycroft (1968) unless otherwise stated.)

others in a group. It can also be particularly effective as a method of cri-sis intervention and is an excellent way of working with those who continue to drink heavily but who are gradually making decisions to change. Despite the fact that counselling can be flexible and useful in a wide range of contexts, the individual counselling format becomes prob-lematic for many problem drinkers.

Most problem drinkers presenting for help feel psychologically and often physically dependent on alcohol. While it is not the case that the majority require a full-blown in-patient detoxification, it is certainly true that many will require a great deal of support, encouragement and advice, especially during the early weeks of abstinence. This is particularly the case for those who are diagnosed with both a mental health and an alco-hol dependency problem. In all of these instances, a counselling session once or even twice a week is likely to be ineffective as it fails adequately to hold clients and support them in their day-to-day and sometimes hour-to-hour struggle to resist alcohol. One session a week is simply not enough for many of those who are newly abstinent.

For those who do find a weekly counselling session sufficient to enable them to stop drinking, other complications arise. When problem drinkers stop drinking they often shift their dependency feelings on to the individuals and organizations that are helping them achieve their goals. They have, after all, denied themselves what was an 'on tap' com-forter and it is understandable that they should seek and hopefully find comfort in newly formed relationships with helping professionals and associations. Prime targets for this form of emotional or 'therapeutic dependency' are AA networks, therapy groups, a hospital or clinic set-ting, or an individual doctor, nurse or counsellor. When newly abstinent clients are offered counselling sessions it is likely that the full brunt of their dependency feelings will become focused on the counsellor and this in turn can create problems. Counsellors, being merely human, fre-quently disappoint or frustrate their clients. Ultimately, they can never compare to the seemingly limitless supply of comfort 'on tap' from alco-hol. Some clients, having started well, relapse in response to their disappointment, sadness or anger when counsellors do not reciprocate deep affections, seem temporarily distracted, irritable or announce plans for a holiday. Alternatively, counsellors who are able to establish a stable, positive, ongoing counselling relationship often find that when they begin to work towards a reduction or termination of sessions, clients become distressed, resist the change and, in many instances, relapse. Counselling is most helpful when advising, supporting or assist-ing individuals in their recognition of an alcohol problem and in helping them to think through and test out a range of response options. It also has a role in working with those who desire or require short bursts of brief contact over time. However, it is an open question whether the use of counselling in the treatment of long-standing alcohol problems is the most effective option for the majority of those needing help to abstain.

Summary

Therapeutic elements

- Provides opportunities for speaking to someone knowledgeable, sympathetic and supportive.
- Provides opportunities for exploring underlying emotional and relationship problems over a period of months or years.
- Provides supportive space for those too timid to attend groups.
- Provides a focused setting for a crisis intervention, when immediate information and/or action are required.

Problematic elements

- One or two meetings a week is inadequate when trying to engage and hold most vulnerable clients who are newly abstinent.
- The counselling process itself runs the risk of drawing intense dependency feelings on to one person (the counsellor) with resultant disappointments and resentments leading to drop-out.
- Absences of the counsellor and termination of counselling often trigger relapse despite preparation.

Day programmes

Day programmes can be found throughout the United Kingdom in both the public and private sectors. Although there are now some Twelve Step day programmes in the UK, most are based on what could loosely be termed a 'psychosocial' model of alcohol dependence. Most offer a range of services that usually include counselling, group therapy and alcohol education, as well as cognitive behavioural interventions such as social skills training, stress management or relapse prevention. Most programmes run for five to eight weeks and require full-time attendance. Some operate ongoing full-time or drop-in programmes where clients can attend for as long as they like and pick and choose such sessions as seem appropriate on any given day.

Day programmes have several advantages over both long-term and short-term residential treatment. They have the potential to offer the support that is characteristic of the therapeutic community and an intensity of experience that appears to be a key factor in achieving early stability, yet they do not require clients to leave their homes or to become separated from ongoing relationships. The trauma of discharge and 're-entry' back into the rigours of everyday life is avoided, or at least the disruptive aspects of the transition are moderated by making the shift between settings into an everyday experience that must be managed in ongoing stages.

Day programmes can also achieve a high degree of flexibility by offering a wide range of interventions, including full-time and part-time attendance for clients who have returned to work or study. Community-based day centres provide an economical, easily accessed setting in which to offer information, advice and treatment to people with drinking problems. However, some individuals find certain aspects of day programme life problematic.

For a start, most centres operate fixed programmes (on average, four to eight weeks of full-time attendance, sometimes followed by a set pattern of part-time attendance) and therefore have the greatest problem associated with residential treatment: abrupt endings. Clients who enter day programmes are usually told that the recovery process does not follow any set pattern, or that each of them is an individual whom experts cannot cure on their own. Although this sounds like an invitation to become active in the treatment process, the fixed nature of most day programme structures (be they full-time or part-time) psychologically hurls individuals straight into a passive relationship where experts prescribe a set course of treatment and clients either follow (good clients) or resist (bad clients) the prescription. For example, a programme may consist of groups every day for six weeks, followed by after-care counselling for six months. Indeed, the concepts of 'follow-up' or 'after-care' covertly communicate that treatment (care) has been successfully completed and that one is now ready to move on. These contradictory overt and covert messages can create a confused passivity in many clients, who all too often relapse just prior to completing a programme or in the early weeks of after-care.

Over the past 10 years, largely in response to these difficulties, some day programmes have begun to operate open structures where clients stay as long as they feel is necessary and can pick and choose which sessions they attend on either a drop-in or an appointment basis. This offers an alternative to the set treatment model and is a step in the right direction. In practice, however, clients are rarely helped to deal with their feelings of dependence and, in particular, how they may express these in attendance choices. They may decide to leave services for all sorts of arbitrary reasons such as boredom in one group or dislike of another client or a confrontation with a staff member whom they would prefer not to work with. Some (favourite) clients continue with programmes for many, many months – in some cases, years – and still fail to deal adequately with their dependency issues and the corresponding vulnerability to relapse. It would seem that those who design day programmes have not yet found ways to incorporate issues relating to dependency, attachment, separation and responsibility into the programme structures themselves. Yet it is these very issues that are therapeutically central to the recovery process and may even be more important than the actual content of sessions or personal disclosures and insights that clients make within them. All too often, clients spend time on day programmes disclosing personal information, expressing previously repressed emotions and learning a lot about recovery, and then relapse because of something unmanageable about the programme structure itself.

Summary

Therapeutic elements

- Provides opportunities for intensive, supportive group experience without requiring clients to leave home.
- Facilitates the readjustment from treatment environment to home environment which is managed each day.
- Provides potential for flexibility of attendance and programme content – full or part-time; day or evening sessions; advice and information; psychodynamic, behavioural, or drop-in, etc.

Problematic elements

- Most programmes are either fixed in content and duration (as in Twelve Step), which fosters passivity, or continue indefinitely, which does not address dependency and separation issues (clients get 'hooked' on treatment).
- Even those programmes offering personal individual timetables do so within a one-to-one, private counselling session (for example, staff member and client prepare a 'treatment plan' for the next month). Most clients don't keep to these individually assessed and agreed programmes, which can result in conflict with staff.

Network and family therapy

Network therapy is based on the premiss that all individuals carry internal maps about their personal experiences and relationships. Behaviour is determined by the way they construct this social reality, and any change in behaviour will occur only within a framework where new information about this reality can be absorbed and considered.

The first aim of the therapy, therefore, is to create a unique, cohesive, supportive network, which then helps each problem drinker to engage and remain engaged in the recovery process. The technique involves mapping out the frame of reference or network in consultation with the drinking client. All important family members, friends or significant others who are connected to the drinker's interrelational system are invited to attend meetings with the therapist in order to work on certain tasks.

The network format is helpful to the problem drinker in several ways:

- It provides explicit and direct education or advice on alcohol problems.
- It provides a forum where both problem drinkers and involved others can develop new coping strategies in response to expected problems.
- It provides opportunities for direct family therapy interventions, which can act to reduce conflict and increase fluidity of roles and potential responses.

Network therapy integrates a range of techniques known to be helpful to problem drinkers such as cognitive behavioural, group and family therapy methods. The original technique (Galanter 1993) has been developed and adapted to include social behaviour and network therapy, as practised in the ongoing UK Alcohol Treatment Trial (UKATT Research Team 2001; Copello et al. 2002). This model is based on the importance of network support for change and also includes elements of the community reinforcement approach (Meyers et al. 1999), and unilateral approaches to drinking problems. Unlike traditional network therapies, work can also be conducted with individuals without non-drinking family or significant others. The first aim of therapy in these circumstances is to develop the network (Copello et al., 2001).

There are good indications that involving family members and others in a supportive system can be extremely helpful to a problem drinker. Not only does membership in a cohesive group seem to increase the drinker's stability of engagement, but it can help in the recovery process by means of directly assisting others closely involved with the drinker to manage their problems and behaviours differently.

Network therapy is a welcome addition to the alcohol intervention repertoire but can pose problems for some problem drinkers. Those who are isolated from any non-drinking networks may be resistant to forming new outside contacts at the commencement of the treatment process. Some may not wish to include family and friends directly, or may have family and friends who do not wish to become involved. Resistance to network involvement is not necessarily a resistance to treatment. Network therapy on its own is not always sufficiently containing for many severe problem drinkers. More often than not, network therapy is offered in conjunction with, or as part of, other interventions such as individual counselling or AA attendance. The combination of approaches can bring new problems associated with other interventions as well as complications arising from 'splitting' between a number of therapists and interventions.

Summary

Therapeutic elements

- Provides a cohesive, support group which increases the likelihood of co-operation and commitment from problem drinkers.
- Provides a forum for direct education, advice and development of coping strategies depending on each member's needs.
- Family interventions help to reduce tensions and facilitate more positive roles and responses.
- A positive emphasis placed on forming support and activity-based community links.

Problematic elements

- Some individuals do not wish to involve family and friends in treatment or have family and friends who do not wish to be involved.
- There is often a need for additional interventions and support that can result in new problems being introduced, including conflict in approach or splitting between different therapists and practices.

CHAPTER 4

Evidence for the effectiveness of treatment

Most experts accept that around 20 to 40 per cent of those problem drinkers who seek help with abstinence manage to achieve their goal and then either abstain or (in the minority of cases) safely control their alcohol intake after leaving treatment. The remainder make a further attempt to get help, stop on their own later, or continue to drink in a damaging way, with the associated psychological and physiological risks. Many of the claims for high success rates – often made by rival treatment services – are based not on follow-up research but on positive and subjective impressions of individual clients by those who have worked with them. Those studies that have taken a more objective look at treatment outcomes have produced some interesting and, at times, curious findings.

For example, there is some evidence to suggest that programmes that incorporate behavioural and family therapy components produce higher success rates than those that do not (Costello 1980; Monahan et al. 1996), but this is so mainly for those with less severe drink problems and for those with close family ties (who tend to do better anyway). For those suffering from particularly entrenched long-term abuse of alcohol, with few social, familial or financial supports, a community-based programme involving direct input on problems such as unemployment seems to contribute to a decrease in abusive drinking (see Heather and Tebbutt 1989, Miller and Hester 1986 and Miller et al. 1995, for reviews of results from over 20 different treatment interventions). Although these findings seem fairly intuitive and straightforward, they cannot be relied upon with a great measure of certainty. Much of the follow-up research is carried out for periods of only three to six months post-treatment, and does not measure what could be seen as long-term stability. We know that for many abstainers uncontained relapses can send them back to the most damaging of drinking patterns. It is the outcome research targeted at two or more years post-treatment that is the most reliable but also, of course, the most difficult and expensive to do.

Some curious findings have been produced from the few long term fol-low-up studies. For example, those that compare minimal intervention treatment (single session counselling, alcohol education sessions or dis-tribution of educational literature) with long-term intensive treatment programmes (Twelve Step or therapeutic community). These show that there is no difference in outcome between the two intensities of approach (Bien et al. 1993; Emrick 1975; Orford and Edwards 1977). Ever since the classic Orford and Edwards study suggested that intensive and expensive treatments were no more effective in the long run than simple, brief inter-ventions, researchers and practitioners have been trying to demonstrate that treatment really does work. The avenue that has been most exten-sively explored over the past 20 years arises from the notion that certain kinds of people respond better to certain kinds of interventions. Out of this idea the eight-year, 27 million dollar American study Project MATCH (Project MATCH Research Group 1993) was born. The central hypothesis of the study was that an individual problem drinker would do better in treatment if his or her personality, aptitudes and cognitive style were matched to particular, relevant interventions.

Within the addiction field the MATCH findings were awaited with great excitement. When they came, the results were stunning, suggesting that matching did not improve outcomes either. Many questions have since been asked. Did the MATCH team select the wrong client attributes to measure, or miss out on a crucial intervention variable? Are the psycho-logical effects inherent in being selected for a high-profile, high-status study more important than the treatment variables themselves, given that all groups showed clear reductions in drinking throughout the intensive three-year follow-up?

The results of Project MATCH did not correspond to the preconceptions of many experts, but this does not mean that some very creative and pro-ductive thinking about treatment has not come out of the study. In fact, the results can be interpreted in several interesting ways. One hypothesis is that it might be a particular intervention *structure* (group vs. individual vs. resi-dential community) as opposed to the particular intervention *content* (Twelve Step vs. cognitive behavioural vs. motivation enhancement) that needs to be matched to a particular section of the dependent population in order to yield different effects. For example, the homeless and rootless may respond particularly well to group-based residential treatment; the newly unemployed to individual counselling and advice; the highly supported and resourced to family or network therapy. Within this framework, those clients not falling within the particular prescribed range would drop away, or other-wise be presented in the statistics as relapses. Project MATCH tested three distinct interventions but provided them within identical structures, i.e. individual counselling, over a twelve-week period, and it therefore could be argued that it is the identical structure of treatment delivery that has yielded near identical outcomes at three-year follow-up. This hypothesis will be partially tested in the upcoming United Kingdom Alcohol Treatment Trial (UKATT) study, which is comparing different structures as well as contents between motivation enhancement therapy (individual counselling) and network therapy (social and familial network groups).

Another interpretation of the findings is that a certain percentage of problem drinkers will respond positively to any form of help as long as (a) it provides them with a non-judgemental space in which to reflect on and define their problem, and work through their ambivalence, and (b) it is delivered by practitioners who are well-trained, skilled, empathic and dedicated (Cartwright 1980). Among this group would be individuals who may have been able to improve or abstain without seeking any kind of formal help at all (Drew 1990; Roizen et al. 1978; Saunders and Kershaw 1979). The remaining problem drinkers do *not* respond positively no matter what help they are offered, in what setting and by whom. This could account for the similar outcomes across treatment groups in Project MATCH.

Whatever our views about interpreting a great amount of sometimes conflicting evidence, it seems to be the case that large numbers of apparently highly motivated, committed individuals voluntarily seek help for their drink problem and then drop out of treatment (be it based on individual or group interventions, day centre or residential settings, Alcoholics Anonymous or psychodynamic approaches). Not only do these starters drop out but they also often fail to respond to letters or telephone calls from the professionals they have worked with and it is probably safe to assume that their silence means they have returned to harmful levels of consumption – for a time, at least. Many of those who do complete a prescribed number of sessions, weeks or months on a given programme usually fall at the hurdle of follow-up or aftercare sessions, leaving the 30 per cent of original starters who can truly be said to have effected lasting change following a specific intervention (Miller and Sanchez-Craig 1996).

Most clinicians will have experience of meeting individuals who simply disappear, often weeks or months after seemingly meaningful and effective work has taken place, and who are never seen again by the same or any other service. For some problem drinkers, this pattern is a crucial part of the recovery process itself, but we know there are many others who continue to go round and round the revolving door for an unnecessarily long number of destructive and painful years. It would be wrong to assume that having opted for an abstinence goal, these individuals do not make a strong commitment to themselves and others to abstain, or that they fail because they are not doing their best within the intervention of their choice. Nonetheless, there is a large group of problem drinkers in any abstinence-based intervention who do repeatedly drop out, or who return to the same or even heavier consumption following the completion of the intervention.

The language of clinicians and researchers often implies that this cycle is the client's failure (treatment resistance of clients), but it is more accurate to describe it as a mismatch between what services and organizations provide and what these particular clients need. This mismatch should be of real concern to clinicians, not least because the research indicates – including findings from Project MATCH – that for many problem drinkers, the longer the contact they have with services, the better the prognosis (Mattson et al. 1998). Indeed, many experts would go so far as to say that it is aftercare that is the crucial variable determining outcome, and not primary treatment experiences at all. If the majority of abstainers coming forward for help either drop out prematurely or never make it into aftercare, regardless of which kinds of interventions are offered, then perhaps the whole notion of abstinence-based treatment needs to be approached in a different way.

One way to tackle this problem is by focusing not on what is working well for those who do well but on what isn't working well for those who break off contact and return to previously harmful drinking patterns, regardless of the orientation or intervention they originally chose. Many clinicians, irrespective of their orientation or preferred style of intervention, have a strong tendency to block out their experiences with 'lost' clients as quickly as possible. It is, after all, easier to attribute a client's unexpected disappearance to inadequate motivation or the like, and to pin hopes and job satisfaction on the survivors who remain engaged or who respond to follow-up questionnaires after they have left treatment. At times it seems as if the clinicians themselves are engaging in the same psychological defence mechanism as that which they attribute to the most disturbed and destructive of their clients, i.e. denial. A more creative strategy is to pay particular attention to those for whom things have not gone well and this is possible to do even after they have broken off contact.

For example, it is very useful to develop a habit of looking back and then noting down what has happened with drop-outs just before they dropped out. In particular, it is important to take note of what could be termed 'last treatment interventions' prior to drop-out. This is done by simply reflecting on what happened yesterday or last week that might have resulted in the individual unexpectedly not showing up for the next session. One can usefully speculate over such questions as these:

- Was that last session experienced as too intense for that person at that time?
- Was the session experienced as too boring or repetitive?

- Were the boundaries or rules of the programme too loose, thereby leading to the client become anxious?
- Were the boundaries too tight, thereby leading to unnecessary authority conflicts with staff?

Sometimes it is the case that a destabilizing event has occurred at home and that this has most likely triggered the relapse or drop-out. Occasionally, the individual did not truly want to settle for abstinence and couldn't say, so simply disappeared. But these instances seem responsible for drop-out only among the minority of those who have opted for and then been properly assessed and prepared for an abstinence treatment option. For most, it seems to be something problematic within the treatment environment itself that has triggered the drop-out.

Arising out of questions about last treatment interventions and the resultant observations and speculations are four features which seem to repeatedly spell trouble for certain clients, no matter what type of service or intervention they are engaged in. Although the problem lies *between* the client and the service, for the sake of simplicity the normal tradition will be followed in reference to characteristics of 'treatment-resistant clients'. It is important to note that while there is some overlap, the list is not identical to findings relating to the group of individuals with alcohol dependency problems as a whole.

The hypothesis, then, is this: *dependent individuals who do well in treatment – or who don't require treatment in order to make and maintain change – are different from equally dependent, equally resourced individuals who do badly in treatment over and over again.*

CHAPTER 5

The features of treatment-resistant clients

Anyone with experience of working with this group will know that no two clients are ever alike. Each individual has his or her own personal history and unique outlook on life and different people have different strengths and skills and, of course, different areas of vulnerability. However, it is my experience that there are four fundamental characteristics that reliably emerge when working with this client group beyond a brief intervention stage, and that have important implications for planning effective treatment interventions.

Therapeutic dependency

The first characteristic concerns the speed and intensity with which therapeutic dependency is formed. Therapeutic dependency is a concept describing the relationship clients may have with professionals when they are engaged in seeking help. It is usually viewed as a fixed (and often ambivalent) attachment to the therapist where clients experience their therapists as crucial to their well-being or even to their survival (Rycroft 1968). Dependency is related to, but not the same as, the therapeutic or working alliance. The alliance refers to the quality of the relationship between patient and therapist, involves empathy, mutual regard and collaboration, and is seen as vital to the efficacy of all psychotherapy (Horvath 1995). The presence of a strong dependency feature is not at all surprising, since upon entering abstinence-based treatment clients have abruptly stopped drinking. Alcohol had provided them with a psychological defence system, offering a partial sense of safety, identity, cohesion and an on-tap psychic pain killer, as well as a source of social, physical and emotional pleasure. It seems reasonable, therefore, that with the termination of drinking, the dependency will transfer to another expected source of emotional comfort such as a doctor, counsellor, day centre or Alcoholics Anonymous activity. This feature often contributes to a problem drinker's ability to stabilize quickly through the link with a particular worker or programme. On the other hand, it is this very same dependency feature which may be responsible for the large numbers of relapses that occur during interruptions due to holidays or illness, or just prior to or following departure from a primary treatment intervention, be it individual-, group- or association-based. Even in those instances where much time and attention has been paid to preparation for leaving primary care programmes, the majority of programme completers do not seem to handle well the transition into aftercare.

Splitting

The second feature is a tendency towards extreme forms of splitting.[1] Treatment-resistant clients often suffer from intense feelings of inferiority and shame, which can shift surprisingly swiftly into an exaggerated and unrealistic confidence, often about their ability to overcome future struggles and temptations to drink. Perceptions about oneself and about others are likely to move rapidly between the extremes of idealization and denigration. This is a feature that is present in all aspects of the individual's life and relationships but can be directly observed in the treatment setting in the form of an overt enthusiasm for the recovery process – the programme is wonderful, the counsellors are wonderful, the client feels good, should have done this years ago, etc. The other side of the split, which is hostility or contempt, is rarely seen in the treatment encounter. It is unusual for the voluntary client to be overtly disruptive, critical or rebellious. More often than not, this side of the personality is invisible to counsellors and other specialists. The client simply disappears and drops out of treatment, often never to return, following an experience which provokes anger or disappointment, and in many cases quickly gets back to abusive levels of consumption. They may later decide to come forward for more help, but this is often with another service, where a similar pattern is likely to be repeated.

---

[1] Splitting is defined within psychoanalytic theory as a defence mechanism. These are developed at a time when the individual does not yet have a mental representation of the self as a single whole, but rather as divided into two or more parts. It is usual for one part to be recognized as the self and the other part to become shut off altogether or experienced as being an attribute of someone else. In most cases, the splits are across polarities such as good/bad, generous/selfish or trustworthy/unreliable and can be experienced as attributes of the self or of others (Rycroft 1968).

Authority issues

The third feature is a preoccupation with boundaries, structures, limits and authority that gives a rather 'adolescent' feel to the therapeutic relationship. The effect of this preoccupation is that staff often get caught up with rules and the implementation of policies around relapse and attendance. Clients get caught up with similar issues – can they argue their way back on to a programme or can they avoid getting caught altogether? Either way, clinicians are pushed into authoritarian stances and clients are not enabled to focus properly and meaningfully on issues of responsibility and choice.

Low tolerance to emotional discomfort

Closely related to the splitting mechanism, the fourth feature of alcohol clients with a history of failure to respond to treatment is a low tolerance to emotional discomfort of all kinds with a particular emphasis on low self-esteem. This means that even moderate amounts of frustration, boredom or anger can trigger a relapse and is precisely why relationships at work and at home have often gone so disastrously wrong in the past. Clients who approach treatment services with the hope that they will learn to manage outside relationships better often find themselves confronted in treatment with the very same problems and feelings that trigger the desire to drink in the first place.

If one accepts the premiss that some or all of the four features are present in those individuals who repeatedly seek help from alcohol services, it is no wonder that they usually fail to do well, or if they do, are unable to leave the services and maintain their stated goals over a significant period of time. In reflecting on the kinds of treatment experiences that are likely to be more effective when working with this group, the summaries of common alcohol interventions (see Chapter 3) should again be considered, bearing the four treatment-resistant characteristics in mind. The PCCP model combines the important therapeutic elements of the seven types of interventions and settings without replicating those elements that may be especially problematic to treatment-resistant clients. However, before describing how the PCCP programme functions and presenting details of its weekly timetable, the following chapter discusses psychoanalytic theory and some of its applications.

CHAPTER 6

Psychoanalytic theory and some of its applications

Psychoanalytic theory has not received much attention in the discussion so far; nevertheless, it has had a fundamental influence on the design of the PCCP model. While a detailed understanding of this material is not a prerequisite for practising the model, a basic understanding of certain core principles is essential. At various points in this chapter there are recommended reading lists for those who want to study a topic in greater detail.

Psychoanalytic theory

Psychoanalysis is not a treatment of choice, or even a useful practice in terms of technique, for the majority of those seeking help for severe alcohol problems. However, the psychoanalytic literature has many interesting things to teach us descriptively about certain kinds of problem drinkers. This is particularly true of the group that would normally experience difficulties with traditional interventions. Freud originally suggested (in a letter to Fliess: Freud 1985) that compulsive drinking was a displacement from the desire to masturbate and focused both on the pleasurable, self-gratifying instincts connected with intoxication and on the aggressive, destructive instincts (Freud 1920). The first published paper on alcoholism (Abraham 1908) linked the problem both to oral fixation and homoerotic sexuality. Other early analysts (Rado 1933; Fenichel 1945), linked alcohol and drug dependence to deficits in self-esteem and to depression arising from the inevitable frustration brought about by unmet oral needs. Within this theoretical framework, alcohol was conceived of as an anaesthetic and was viewed more as a failed defence mechanism than as an expression of a destructive or pleasurable drive.

Psychoanalytic theory specifically relating to addiction problems has come a long way from early conceptions about oral fixation and

unresolved dependency needs associated with the intra-psychic model of
libido theory (Freud 1917).[1] Recent contributions have changed the frame
from one of a closed system to that of an open, interpersonal one. Within
the object relations school,[2] the individual is viewed as a point within a
social/psychological network where notions of self and identity (and con-
sequent behaviour) are predominantly determined by early relationships.
Within this theoretical perspective, substance misuse is viewed as a partial
solution to inadequacies within the self that have been caused by trauma
or deficits in early relationships. The way we come to understand our-
selves is viewed as determined primarily by our personal models of
relationships. These models gradually become our internalized (intra-psychic) structures or maps about the world and the people in it.

While few contemporary clinicians work with substance misusers within the individual psychoanalytic setting, there are two whose ideas have
had an impact on the development of the PCCP model. In a paper about
the psychodynamics of drug dependency, Limentani (1986) describes substance misuse primarily as an attempt to deal with conflict surrounding
aggression. He also links the drug-taking experience with sexuality by suggesting that the drive towards satiation through drug use can be
understood as a parallel drive towards sexual satiation.

Hopper (1995), who has postulated the existence of an 'addiction syndrome', has explored this theme further. He suggests that the root of all
addiction is located in early trauma, which in turn triggers the need to
engage in certain kinds of fantasies and practices (predominantly sexual
and particularly homosexual) as a means of deriving comfort from frightening aggressive feelings. He makes a further link between trauma,
homosexual fantasies and risk-taking behaviour.

Whether or not substance misuse practitioners find these kinds of formulations useful, some themes have particular relevance in day-to-day
clinical work even within the most non-analytic of settings. For example,
the notion of alcohol as an anaesthetic has real implications for the way
we understand a client's needs and behaviour. The emphasis on intense
anxiety surrounding aggression and its expression seems particularly
important when considering what kinds of experiences newly abstinent
substance misusers should and should not be exposed to in treatment.

---

[1] Libido theory defines thought processes and behaviour as predominantly determined by impulses relating to sexual energy and drives (Rycroft 1968).

[2] Psychoanalytic theory defines an object as anything 'towards which an action or
desire is directed' (Rycroft 1968: 100). In practice, an object almost always refers to a
person or a part of a person. Object relations theory refers to the school within psychoanalytic theory where an individual's need to relate to others is viewed as more
crucial to determining behaviour than is the need to reduce instinctual, physiological
pressure and conflict.

There is also a strong implication in the writings that men and women have different unconscious reasons for taking drugs, different needs from treatment, and different experiences of treatment. Most clinicians would concur that men and women do tend to use groups and counselling somewhat differently (Alonso and Rutan 1979; Blazina 2001). Whereas most women find it relatively easy to make intimate (at times, premature) connections and disclosures in therapy, many men find it awkward, despite recent social and cultural influences that encourage more intimate, emotion-laden exchanges from men. In terms of gender identity conflict, men may unconsciously associate speaking about the internal world with femininity, which may consequently arouse strong anxieties in some (Elliott 1986). Understanding needs and experiences across and between the sexes is a complex personal, social and cultural endeavour. While most substance misuse practitioners would not find these psychoanalytic formulations directly appropriate to their clinical setting, some of the ideas arising from individual psychoanalytic sessions may help practitioners to think through these important issues with increased depth.

Although he did not specialize in working with substance misusers, the psychoanalyst often cited and closely associated with the treatment of substance misuse is Heinz Kohut (1977). Kohut's theoretical framework, referred to as 'self psychology', focuses on the individual's struggle to experience him or herself as a separate, cohesive being in relation to others. The ability to 'integrate and organize fragmenting affect into meaningful experience' (Flores 2001) is fundamental to achieving this aim. For those who, due to early deprivations and traumas, are unable to build a reliable 'psychic structure' (Kohut) based on a sense of themselves as cohesive, genuine and consistent, a partial yet inadequate solution is to take mood-altering drugs (Levin 1987, Weegmann 2002). Drugs create certain emotions and comforting fantasies about the self and the self in the world. In particular, drugs such as alcohol can create an illusion of being in control of oneself and others, and a sense of being connected or merged with objects (others) in the world. Psychoanalytic theory views fantasy about control and connectedness as a process of normal, healthy development in the individual, referred to in the literature as 'healthy narcissism'. However, healthy development also involves the gradual relinquishing of fantasies about control and this, it is argued, is what is not satisfactorily achieved by those who go on to use drugs habitually. Within Kohut's model, the psychological pain associated with pathological narcissism and the resultant 'disorders of the self' is temporarily relieved by the creation of omnipotent fantasies, through the effects of mood-altering drugs.

What Kohut is describing is a process whereby alcohol or drug use becomes a means of self-medicating. The effects of the alcohol bring with them a sense of control, well-being and confidence in oneself, almost as if one has gained magical powers. The discomfort arising out of problems in self-regulation and the modulation of feelings and impulses is what triggers the desire to self-medicate. This important conceptual break-through has enabled others such as Edward Khantzian (Khantzian et al. 1990) to use Kohut's ideas as a basis for creating innovative treatment programmes designed specifically for substance misusers.

Khantzian (1981, 1990), whose ideas closely reflect the development of psychoanalytic thought from instinct to ego function, postulates two main impairments in ego functioning occurring in substance misusers:

1. A lack of *self care*. This is understood as a failure in sensitivity to, or awareness of, danger to the self or, if registered, a lack of concern or fear about it.
2. An inability to regulate feelings or often even to identify or verbalize them. This failure can lead to affect which is both overwhelming and undifferentiated, resulting in panic, rage or, in extreme cases, psychosis (Krystal 1982).

Within the Khantzian framework, substance misusers are unable to regulate their feelings and are therefore at constant risk of becoming overwhelmed by them. Because prolonged unmanageable affect can lead to trauma, individuals turn to alcohol (and other drugs) as a means of coping with what feels like threatening, unbearable pain. In this way, alcohol is used not primarily to gratify infantile wishes and drives but in an attempt to feel better about the self. Soothing the self is something that substance misusers are unable to do for themselves or with any consistency within a relationship. Rather than seeing it as a destructive impulse, Khantzian describes substance misuse as the individual's attempt to solve problems:

> ... substance-dependent persons suffer and self medicate not only because they do not know, tolerate or express their feelings but also because they cannot regulate their self esteem, relationships or self care.
>
> (Khantzian 1997: 250)

Although Kohut's psychoanalytic model is, more than any other, associated with the treatment of substance misusers, it is the theory of Borderline Personality Disorder (BPD) and, in particular, Otto Kernberg's work on Borderline Personality Organization (Kernberg 1975) that has most influenced the structure of the PCCP model. The concept of BPD, originating in the 1930s, has been a controversial and confusing one but, largely due to the work of Kernberg, there has been considerably more agreement about definitions over the past 30 years. Borderline patients have aspects to their personalities that are consistent with elements found in both the neuroses and psychoses, but are conceptualized as structurally different and separate from both. Like Kohut's ideas about disorders of the self, the fundamental unifying feature of BPD is that a stable, integrated, consistent and cohesive ego structure has not been developed. This, in turn, creates a severe disturbance in the processes of individuation and separation (Jackson et al. 1986). Because a secure ego structure is not in place, the individual cannot effectively rely on the normal, healthy range of defence mechanisms such as repression, regression or displacement.[3] He or she must therefore rely heavily on the more primitive defence mechanisms of projection, introjection and projective identification,[4] and this has a great effect on day-to-day relationships. Borderline patients time and time again resort to primitive splitting defences in their attempts to defend themselves against what feels like unmanageable and unbearable psychic pain. Not only is the world experienced as a series of fragmented extremes – populated by heroes and villains – but the individuals themselves, in resorting to these defences, suffer from the fragmentation of their own egos and identities. This accounts for the severe mood swings that are such a predominant feature of this group.

Individuals diagnosed with BPD usually suffer greatly from a sense of insecurity and a lack of self-esteem, which strangely runs in parallel with grandiosity, superiority, and a sense of omnipotence. They tend to have a low tolerance for emotional pain (frustration, anger, depression, boredom) and are extremely sensitive to criticism and feelings of rejection. Their relationships tend to be one-sided rather than mutual. In working with them clinically, one often has the sense of not being recognized as

---

[3] Within psychoanalytic theory, defence mechanisms are unconscious and come into operation automatically to protect the ego (sense of self) from unmanageable conflict, anxiety or other threats to equilibrium. Repression occurs when an unacceptable impulse or thought is made unconscious and therefore is unknown to the self. Regression occurs when anxiety or conflict is avoided by reverting back to an earlier and more primitive state of functioning or thinking. Displacement occurs when energy and interest is moved from one person or activity to a less anxiety-provoking more acceptable person or activity.

[4] Projection occurs where 'impulses, wishes or aspects of the self are imagined to be located in some object external to the self' (Rycroft 1968: 126), as when one denies a feeling or wish but attributes it to someone else. Introjection occurs where the attributes of an existing person or thing, are imagined to be inside the self. Projective identification occurs where unwanted aspects of the self are split off and experienced as being located in someone else. As part of the ongoing relationship with that person, the aspects or impulses are held and transformed until they can be eventually taken back and recognized as belonging to the self, a concept which forms a link between one's thoughts and feelings and other people (Ogden 1979).

separate but rather as being viewed as an extension of themselves and used accordingly to support a precariously weakened sense of self.

As a result of the persistent threat of unmanageable pain – a fear of falling apart and of being literally shattered into pieces, these individuals' lives become more and more centred around pain avoidance. This view is consistent with the 'self-medication' hypothesis, and repeated, dependent use of alcohol as a form of psychic anaesthetic provides the conceptual link between borderline states and drug dependency.

Those working with treatment-resistant problem drinkers will be familiar with many of the psychiatric features associated with BPD as listed in *DSM-IV*:

1. Self-destructive impulsivity or unpredictability (for example, substance abuse, shoplifting, over-eating, self-mutilation)
2. Unstable and intense interpersonal relationships (for example, idealization, devaluation, manipulation, marked shifts of attitude)
3. Inappropriate, intense anger or lack of control of anger
4. Identity disturbance manifested by uncertainty about issues such as self-image, gender identity, values, career choice, loyalties
5. Instability of mood (marked shifts from normal mood to depression, irritability or anxiety usually lasting a few hours and only rarely more than a few days
6. Intolerance of being alone
7. Physically self-damaging acts (suicidal gestures, recurrent accidents, or physical fights)
8. Chronic feelings of emptiness or boredom.

(American Psychiatric Association 1994)

Despite some overlap, individuals who fit the criteria for Alcohol Dependence Syndrome (Edwards and Gross 1976) are not an identical population to those who fit the psychiatric criteria for BPD. However, the four features outlined in Chapter 5 that are associated with treatment-resistant clients are not dissimilar to many of the characteristics and affects described in the psychoanalytic literature on BPD. It is one of the assumptions underlying the PCCP model that it is those problem drinkers who either fit the criteria of BPD or who have some similar, or less severe features, who are the same individuals who go around the 'revolving door' of alcohol services, never managing to achieve stability for very long. This hypothetical link between borderline type features and treatment-resistant clients is important for the clinician to hold in mind when working with the PCCP model as it informs appropriate culture formation and individual interactions within daily practice.

Group analytic theory

It is not altogether surprising that, with this range of presenting characteristics, most psychoanalysts, individual analytic psychotherapists, and counsellors have turned away from working with those troubled by addiction problems (for some exceptions, see Arroyave 1986; Hopper 1995; Limentani 1986; Rodriquez de la Sierra 2002; Rosenfeld 1960), and there is no doubt that the professional substance misuse field in the United Kingdom is dominated by counsellors offering cognitive behavioural interventions.

Individual analytic counselling and psychotherapy is certainly hard to establish and harder to maintain with this group of clients. To begin with, most of them are not able to establish a firm therapeutic alliance based on the 'as if' aspect vital in transference interpretations. In fact, interpretations are usually experienced as criticisms or attacks. Clients are very easily wounded, and the stresses inherent in meaningful psychotherapy (including the working through of depression) cannot be tolerated and often, in themselves, trigger relapse. Because of the over-use of splitting (involved in projective identification), the attitude towards the therapist often moves quickly from a highly idealized one to one of a hated and dangerous persecutor. This, in turn, precipitates either relapse or abrupt termination of therapy or, usually, both.

Although some specific techniques have been developed to facilitate the individual therapy of patients who have borderline-type symptoms (Kernberg et al. 1989; Leighton 1997), a good way to move beyond the many problems of working individually with patients who have borderline type symptoms is to work exclusively with them in groups (Pines 1978; Roller and Nelson 1999; Weldon 1994). Groups suit treatment-resistant problem drinkers far better than one-to-one interventions for a number of reasons. Some of these have been described as curative or therapeutic factors (Yalom 1975) and include the following: installation of hope, universality, imparting of information, altruism, development of socializing techniques and interpersonal learning. Group life provides endless opportunities for mutual identification, support and sharing, all of which can contribute to a sense of increased self-esteem and containment within the individual. As well as providing intensely profound intra-personal and interpersonal experiences, there also occur more relaxed, neutral experiences. Clients can gain a sense of being in relationship with others in ways that feel expressive of, without being hazardous to, the self.

But the most important reason why groups should be the treatment of choice for this client group is that relationships with therapists – and others – are much easier to manage over time – and recovery from dependency problems does take time. For example, when the inevitable intensely negative feelings are experienced towards the therapist, other group members can be taken up as allies who may even share the same point of view. This in turn makes the negativity more bearable and thus the therapy process itself is much less likely to turn sour. By surviving the crisis of negative feelings in combination with more neutral or positive feelings, problem drinkers are slowly helped to integrate diverse parts of themselves and others. As ambivalence becomes possible and then tolerable, an acceptance of the good and bad in the self and in others becomes stronger and more stable. If patients can be held in a group programme over time, they have repeated opportunities for building up and internalizing new and more robust psychological structures. This, in turn, fosters an increased ability to manage emotional pain and hence an increase in stability. Group work is now recognized by many substance misuse specialists as fundamental to the recovery process, but in most cases (and unlike the PCCP model) is advocated in conjunction with AA attendance and/or individual counselling.

The range of group sessions offered on the PCCP day programme is a mixture of cognitive, behavioural, activity-based and analytic, psychodynamic approaches. The major influence on the model as a whole, however, comes directly from group-analytic theory (Foulkes 1948, 1964). Within group-analytic practice, group members are free to determine the content and pace of sessions without direction or interference from the group analyst. This self-directed activity takes place within tightly controlled boundaries that are defined and carefully maintained by the analyst at all times. This practice of maintaining clear boundaries and procedures is referred to by Foulkes as 'dynamic administration' and is a key concept in the day-to-day operation of the PCCP model. In practice, client self-determination within clearly defined boundaries and practices enables clinicians to remain non-interfering and supportive in response to choices individuals make about their treatment programmes. Examples of how this self-determination becomes actualized in day-to-day practice are found in the following chapter, which describes the model in detail.

For further reading on groups and the treatment of substance misuse, see the following: Flores 1997, 2001; Khantzian 2001; Khantzian et al. 1990; Matano and Yalom 1991; Stevenson and Ruscombe-King 1993; Vanicelli 1982, 1992, 2001; Yalom 1975.

Therapeutic community theory

Another important influence on the thinking behind the PCCP structure comes from the literature on the early therapeutic community movement of the 1940s and 1950s. Therapeutic communities, traditionally in-patient, were originally established to help disturbed individuals who would otherwise have ended up in prison or psychiatric hospitals. There have now been so many applications and alterations to the original practice that it is more useful to think of the therapeutic community as a 'treatment modality rather than a treatment model' (Kennard 1998a). The key to the therapeutic effect revolves around the creation of a close-knit community of patients and staff where the core therapeutic medium is viewed as communication about and analysis of day-to-day events, rather than formal 'therapy' sessions.

Many of the original features have little in common with current approaches to residential rehabilitation for alcohol problems today, or with 'Concept Houses', created in the United States as a means of treating illicit drug use. However, a few of the founding principles are fundamental to an understanding about the kind of culture and experience that leads to recovery within the PCCP model.

First, the emphasis on a close-knit group of clients and staff working together not only facilitates a good ongoing understanding of how each client is progressing but also enables the clinical team to work closely together in the management of problems, conflicts and splits among clients, which are often played out in relation to staff.

Another important principle stems from the curiously practical and down-to-earth perspective which underpinned the early work in this field, despite the fact that most of the pioneers in the Therapeutic Community movement were practising psychoanalysts: Wilfred Bion, Tom Main and S.H. Foulkes amongst others. The ideas of Maxwell Jones, who did not advocate the development of increasingly sophisticated forms of psychotherapy, particularly embody this straightforward approach. He stressed that the chief aim of any therapeutic community was to help individuals to 'organize their own lives' (Foster 1979: 281) by making increasingly better adjustments to outside family, work and social relationships (Jones 1956). Towards this aim, he stressed the importance of involvement by all members of the community in community decisions, peer group support and the striving towards autonomy and independence for patients.

The combination of intense and active involvement by clients in the treatment process, together with peer group support and attention to authority and boundary issues, is fundamental to the understanding of the PCCP model. It is the commitment to explore relationships and feelings for the purpose of retrieving and building new links with outside family, social and work networks that is vital to what can be viewed as therapeutic. It is therefore crucial that, at the same time as gaining insight into how they relate to others within the community, clients are encouraged to go out and initiate work/social/educational links outside the community as an *equal* part of the therapeutic experience.

For further reading on therapeutic communities, see the following: Hinshelwood 1987; Kennard 1998b; Whiteley and Gordon 1979.

Attachment theory

Attachment is explored under the umbrella of social, learning and psychoanalytic theories and provides a framework for understanding individuals and their relationships throughout life. The core idea spelled out by Bowlby (1953, 1969), and developed by Robertson (1958), Ainsworth (1989) and others, is that, from birth, the relationship that exists between the baby and its mother (or other primary carer) sets expectations of the world and the people in it.

All babies and young children have an innate, biological tendency to seek out or attract the attention of their most important carers (attachment figures) whenever they become uncomfortable, uneasy or distressed. Their aim is to get close to those who can bring relief, and towards this aim they instinctually engage in predictable kinds of behaviour. These behaviours are their attempts to draw attention to their needs. Within the conceptual model, there is an equally strong instinctual pull from primary carers to respond to the signals and so, within a normal mother–child relationship, a good match or emotional dialogue is achieved. The instinctual behaviours of the infant can take several forms:

- signalling behaviour such as smiling
- aversive behaviours such as crying
- active behaviours such as crawling towards an attachment figure.

Attachment theory states that any situation that elicits anxiety triggers one of the three attachment behaviours. In normal, healthy circumstances, mothers and babies are predisposed to respond to one another until the anxiety or discomfort is sufficiently managed. In situations where mothers are not accessible or sensitive to attachment behaviour, babies become increasingly disturbed and as a result develop defensive strategies that enable them to cope with their discomfort. If the bond between mother and baby is inconsistent, inflexible or abruptly broken off, a pattern of relating is established which brings with it problematic behaviours and corresponding relationship difficulties.

These infant behaviours and mothers' responses to them not only provide for infants' physical needs but also help infants to develop a picture of the world and their place within it. The qualities of this internalized map depend on the earliest experiences of the mother's availability, responsiveness and consistency in caretaking. Within these earliest attachment relationships, babies not only learn about the world but also begin to recognize patterns of emotion and then to learn how to translate and regulate them.

Attachment theory originally described three, but has now been expanded to include four, distinct patterns or strategies for relating to others. The theory suggests that most individuals favour one strategy as their predominant style, particularly during times of stress. These are:

- *Secure* attachments: where individuals experience themselves as basic-ally good and able to communicate their needs clearly to others, who are experienced as largely responsive.
- *Avoidant/rejecting* attachments: where individuals experience them-selves as unloved and self-reliant and others are experienced as unresponsive.
- *Avoidant/fearful* attachments: where individuals experience them-selves as essentially bad and others are experienced as frightening and unavailable.
- *Preoccupied/ambivalent* attachments: where individuals experience themselves as dependent, with low self-esteem and others are experi-enced as unreliable or neglecting.

The later three defensive patterns are developed in response to early environmental deprivation or abuse and then become the habitual style of relating to new situations and relationships. The patterns, together with their associated rules, become internalized maps of the social world and there is a strong correlation between early attachment strategies and adult behaviour. In relation to those with alcohol problems, it is clear that avoidant patterns do not mix well with ongoing treatment interventions. Those who do engage in predominantly avoidant behaviours are hard to engage in any kind of treatment beyond brief intervention or drop-in ser-vices. Within ongoing treatment settings, it is the preoccupied/ambivalent behaviours that cause the most difficulty, particularly among those who begin well but then break off or relapse at the conclusion of an interven-tion. Those showing predominantly ambivalent attachment styles tend to have deep anxieties about their self-worth and capacity to be loved. They have a tendency to become enmeshed in relationships (which sometimes are mistaken for a desire to work deeply in therapy) and although they seek attention and intimacy, they are easily angered or disappointed in the responses they receive from clinicians (carers). As the label suggests, they are preoccupied with doubts about whether those to whom they would want to turn in time of need will be available and consistent. And these are the very individuals who experience rejection when clinicians go on holiday or when it is time to separate from them and the primary treat-ment setting.

Relevance of psychoanalytic theories to the PCCP model

The PCCP model is not psychoanalytic. In practice, however, all of the examples and applications of psychoanalytic theory outlined above contribute directly to the structure of the weekly programme. Both Kohut's and Kernberg's concepts of fragmentation and deficits in the self point to therapeutic community and/or group work as the treatment of choice. It is within the group setting that treatment-resistant individuals have a good chance of becoming attached to an interpersonal network that is both engaging and containing. The very process of immersion into a group culture elicits a quality of affect that functions as a direct substitute for drug-taking behaviour (Flores 2001). The engagement in group life facilitates attachments to the group as a whole that enable the setting to function as a kind of 'transitional object' (Winnicott 1971). Transitional objects, objects such as a favourite teddy bear or blanket, have a fundamental role in early psychological development. They are defined by Winnicott as being located somewhere between the infant's internal world and the external social reality. Within this area of intermediate space, the infant is free to manipulate and largely control certain elements as a means of deriving comfort, while at the same time maintaining links with others through play or dialogue. The use the individual makes of this space has a fundamental influence on adult behaviour and the use one makes of others in relationships.

Substance misuse treatment has long been recognized by many clinicians as a 'time-dependent' process (Flores 2001, citing Wallace 1978 and Washton 1992). There are clearly defined treatment tasks during different phases in the individual's contact. At its most basic, early priorities are concerned with achieving abstinence and require containment, active support, advice and education. Later phases are concerned with avoiding relapse, which is largely achieved through the gradual resolution of splits and deficits that have previously triggered unmanageable emotions leading to substance misuse and dependency. An increased ability to identify and communicate emotions to others is seen as the first step towards internal containment. While many clinicians have identified the need to move individuals through appropriate phase-specific treatment, the PCCP model places a particular emphasis on phased, seamless, client-directed movement. Not only are movement and sequence fundamental to the programme, but specific mechanisms have been explicitly developed which place each individual at the centre of the process. Inherent in the programme structure is the notion that self-control and active decision-making run hand-in-hand with self-efficacy and commitment. Having accepted that substance abusers are experts at knowing how to regulate their emotions by self-medicating procedures (Khantzian et al. 1990), we can now introduce them into a culture where they must quickly become expert at self-prescribing treatment for themselves on a regular weekly basis. Just as the creative use of transitional objects is a fundamental task for any infant, the discovery of movement, control and creative use of the programme itself is at the heart of the client's task within the PCCP model. It is this task above all others that is viewed as fundamentally curative. With these elements and applications of psychoanalytic theory in mind, it is now time to consider the PCCP weekly timetable.

CHAPTER 7

The Monday to Friday programme

The dual focus of the PCCP model

While complex in terms of its theoretical underpinnings, the programme itself is designed to be straightforward in terms of structure. It focuses on two fundamental aims but this dual focus, while appearing simple, is deceptively difficult to achieve:

Focus 1: To engage and contain recently abstinent and, in many cases, highly unstable, chaotic clients in a day centre setting until a degree of physical and psychological stability is achieved.

Focus 2: To enable each client to take full and active ongoing responsibility for decisions about the content of their treatment and their weekly programme as well as outside activities and commitments. This includes facilitating a negotiated departure from the day programme and on to aftercare.

The clinical emphasis is on structure (how it works) rather than on the content of individual sessions, which with a few exceptions is of little importance. A good guiding principle in designing a PCCP timetable is to have a fair mix of cognitive, psychodynamic and activity-based sessions. With the exception of the Friday timetable, most of the decisions about what groups to offer throughout the week should be determined by individual staff members' interests, enthusiasms and skills.

Many abstinence-based treatment programmes seek to offer very full days with a wide range of daily session choices provided by many different sessional and part-time staff. At first glance this looks attractive and engaging, but clients offered a multitude of options and therapies can become over-stimulated and overwhelmed at the beginning of a new treatment experience. More importantly, a group of clients that has split up into different parallel session options does not have the opportunity to form as one cohesive working group that is fundamental to a well-functioning therapeutic community. Similarly, 'pick and mix' or 'drop-in' programmes are often not sufficiently stabilizing to hold newly abstinent clients who encounter groups made up of different people at different stages of recovery every time they attend.

Although simple in appearance, the PCCP programme is designed to directly counteract these difficulties as well as the problems and conflicts arising from each of the four characteristics of treatment-resistant clients outlined above. In designing a timetable, the emphasis on *structure* rather than *content* cannot be stressed enough. How clients make use of the programme as a whole and in parts, how they settle into it, how they manage to move away from it and what they move on to replace it with, is what matters most at all times in the treatment process.

The finalized full-time timetable of no more than ten weekly groups is relatively simple for new clients to absorb yet contains mechanisms within the structure which will enable each individual to create a custom-made programme by their third week. This programme will be uniquely geared towards individual preferences and therapeutic abilities. Clients learn how to design personal timetables of varying intensity from full-time to a few hours a week depending on personality and mood, outside commitments and stage of recovery. Although this programme is deliberately less busy than that of many other day programmes, when considering effectiveness and long-term stability less may, in this case, be more.

Monday	Tuesday	Wednesday	Thursday	Friday
10.00 Open	10.00 Open	10.00 Open	10.00–12.30 Closed to clients Half day (staff meetings)	9.30 Open
11.00–12.30 Open discussion group	11.00–12.30 Art therapy	11.00–12.30 Yoga class		10.00–11.45 Clients review 12.15–1.15 Community group
12.30–1.30 Lunch break	12.30–1.30 Lunch break	12.30–1.30 Lunch break	12.30–1.30 Lunch break	1.15–2.30 Lunch break
1.30–3.00 Alcohol/drug education seminar	1.30–3.00 Men's and women's groups	1.30–3.00 Anxiety management/assertiveness group	1.30–3.00 Relapse prevention group	2.30–4.00 Activity/Personal development
6.00–7.30 Second stage	5.30–7.00 Second stage	6.00–7.30 Second stage	3.30–5.00 Second stage	Close
	6.00–7.30 Second stage		6.30–8.00 Second stage	

Figure 7.1 Example of a PCCP day programme timetable

There are four therapeutic aims contained within the programme timetable that are worked on throughout the week. These are concerned with containment/stability, education, insight and separation/responsibility.

Therapeutic element I: containment/stability

Objectives: to create a therapeutic environment which offers sufficient structure to hold clients through the fragile and often volatile stages of early abstinence. The primary concern is to achieve a balance of sessions so that clients are not over-stimulated or confronted with emotions they cannot yet tolerate, yet are not bored or restless.
Session examples: yoga/relaxation; art class; activities group (also designed to link directly into outside interests and activities).

Therapeutic element II: education

Objectives: to provide a range of sessions which approach alcohol problems cognitively and behaviourally, thereby enabling clients to actively engage in learning how to recover.
Session examples: alcohol education group; anxiety management; assertiveness; relapse prevention.

Therapeutic element III: insight

Objectives: to provide a range of sessions where clients can explore and gain understanding into both outside and inside relationship issues as well as those current problems for which they may be seeking support.
Session examples: open discussion group, art therapy, single gender groups.

Therapeutic element IV: separation/responsibility

Objectives: to facilitate and encourage the shift away from an early position of heightened dependency to a position of increasing responsibility and decision-making. The focus is on the client taking control of treatment content, including important decisions about when and how to wean off from the day programme and into evening aftercare. This should always be achieved in conjunction with taking up work or other outside activities.
Session examples: review meeting, community group.

In order to create a custom-built version of the PCCP timetable, clinicians must have considerable clarity about which sessions are flexible and open to alteration and which sessions are fundamental to the model itself. The following timetable illustrates which sessions are fundamental and provides some alternative suggestions for the remaining groups. While sessions such as 'stress management', 'education' or 'relapse prevention' are not germane to the PCCP approach, their presence in the weekly timetable is generally recommended.

Monday	Tuesday	Wednesday	Thursday	Friday
10.00 Open	10.00 Open	10.00 Open	10.00–12.30 Closed to clients Half day (staff meetings)	9.30 Open
11.00–12.30 Session 1	11.00–12.30 Session 3	11.00–12.30 Session 5		10.00–11.45 Clients review
				12.15–1.15 Community group
12.30–1.30 Lunch break	12.30–1.30 Lunch break	12.30–1.30 Lunch break	12.30–1.30 Lunch break	1.15–2.30 Lunch break
1.30–3.00 Session 2	1.30–3.00 Session 4	1.30–3.00 Session 6	1.30–3.00 Session 7	2.30–4.00 Activity/Personal development
6.00–7.30 Second stage	5.30–7.00 Second stage	6.00–7.30 Second stage	3.30–5.00 Second stage	Close
6.30–8.00 Monthly family and friends information and support	6.00–7.30 Second stage		6.30–8.00 Second stage	

Figure 7.2 Alternative day programme timetable

Some alternative group choices (sessions 1–7): psychodrama; music appreciation; creative writing; cooking classes; gardening; arts and crafts; weaving; looking at childhood; plans for the future; tai chi; themed group; working on loss; making new relationships.

CHAPTER **8**

How the day programme works

Anyone wishing to attend the day programme is required, and must agree, to attend all ten weekly sessions for a minimum of two weeks. This compulsory period functions as an anchor and stabilizes new clients, who usually begin to feel 'at home' in their new environment midway through the second week. At the end of this period, depending on how the client feels and what they have learned about fellow clients' early experiences, they may wish to consider a gradual reduction, dropping a session or two, leading to their own tailor-made part-time programme. This is reviewed weekly so that clients have an opportunity to make adjustments if they have cut down prematurely or made mistakes about what kinds of groups will be most helpful to them at particular times. At the other extreme, if they are anxious about cutting down at all, they can begin to tackle the reduction gradually with the support of their peers and staff in the Friday review and community group.

There are two mechanisms in the programme that have been specific-ally designed to promote stability and containment on the one hand and the development of responsibility and separation on the other. These are the Friday morning compulsory sessions and the Second Stage structure. These elements represent the key structural components of the model (see Figure 8.1).

Compulsory sessions on Friday morning

The review meeting

All clients must attend the Friday review meeting throughout their stay on the day programme. All core staff members will also be present including the administrator, who records a summary of each individual's review. Within a two-hour session, a maximum of 24 clients have up to a five-

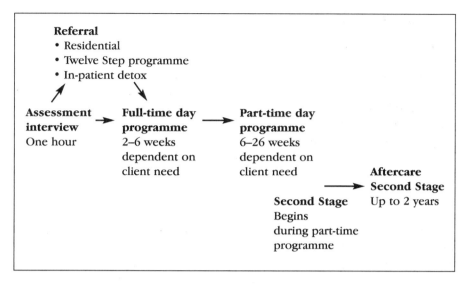

Figure 8.1 The phased PCCP programme

minute review, one at a time. Each individual begins by assessing perceived progress (or lack of it) during the week in relation to self-defined aims. Each client then receives two or three pieces of brief feedback from peers and/or staff about what the client has said (or any relevant observations from the week). The client then designs a treatment programme for the following week depending on the client's assessment of how he or she is (how many groups to do) and what he or she thinks needs to be worked on (which sessions to select). Individual reviews end with the client stating a focus or aim on which to concentrate for the next seven days. All comments are written up in the meeting and transcribed on to a paper which is brought back to the Review Group the following Friday and read out before the client begins with a new assessment of the past week.

This highly structured large group meeting embodies and represents the overriding commitment to clients' decision-making power. It functions against a backdrop of staff and clients collectively reflecting on each individual and thereby enabling them to consider and then to make meaningful treatment choices (Moos et al. 1990). The process in itself provides focused containment and facilitates self-motivation, self-efficacy and active responsibility for day-to-day treatment options. The use of the written notes or 'contracts' carried over from week to week provides continuity and also highlights periods of progress or lack of it, be it practical or emotional. The unique structure of the Review Group holds the programme together for those who are part-time and enables all 24 clients to feel actively involved in the community and in one another's treatment decisions.

Example of review for Joan B

Review of the week

Joan said she has been feeling terrible over the past couple of days. She found it strange hearing her review from last Friday because everything seemed to be going so well and she was feeling very optimistic about staying away from drinking. She feels particularly down today because she has no plans for the weekend and knows it is dangerous for her to sleep late and just sit around all day. She doesn't really have much else to say – it's just a bad day.

Feedback from group

Jack wanted to remind Joan that it is normal to have mood changes and she needs to get through it. It is important for her to hold on to the fact that she was feeling good a few days ago and will feel good again soon.

Fred suggested that Joan try to give herself a treat for the weekend. Maybe go to a movie. Even though she doesn't like AA, it is better to go and chat to people there than to pick up a drink.

Sue suggested that Joan come in to the clinic more next week than she did this week. Maybe she cut down her attendance too much too soon.

Timetable for next week

Monday, a.m.
Tuesday, all day.
Wednesday, p.m. (attends adult education art class in the morning).
Thursday, p.m.
Friday, a.m.

Focus

To try to remember she has felt better and will feel better again and to promise herself she will ring her cousin tonight and plan something nice to do over the weekend with her.

The Community Group

The PCCP Community Group operates in many respects like that of any other community meeting in a therapeutic community setting. It provides a forum where all clients and staff will meet together to share information, make announcements, discuss day-to-day community business and debate topical issues. It is also a space where underlying and often unconscious themes are free to surface and can then be articulated and explored.

Unlike many therapeutic communities, however, the PCCP community meeting takes place only once a week and follows on from the Review Meeting on a Friday morning. The review structure is tight and does not allow for any in-depth exploration or lengthy dialogue between clients. The Community Group acts as a container for any unresolved emotion (especially conflict) arising out of the review process itself. It also enables the community to focus on any clients who are arousing concern following their review and offer direct additional support and advice.

Friday afternoon activities session

The Friday afternoon activities group is not a compulsory session yet it is an important part of the PCCP model and is the only group that clients can opt into without notice. On the surface, the activities group has straightforward and simple aims. It provides an opportunity for clients to engage in and learn new activities and hobbies that can be taken up at home. These include painting, work with clay or wood, model-making, knitting, embroidery, calligraphy, weaving, jewellery-making or any other activity that can be contained within one large room or studio. The activities group also provides an opportunity for clients to engage in a game of Scrabble, Trivial Pursuit or cards, which can come as a welcome relief following the focus and intensity of the morning sessions. By introducing an opportunity to take up neutral tasks, which can be done alone or in small groups, clients are both distracted from any emotional discomfort which may have been aroused in the morning sessions and contained together within a safe, non-threatening group environment. A sense of containment is particularly important for clients to achieve prior to leaving the programme on Friday afternoon.

The activities group is also the last chance for staff to observe any client who may be arousing concern. Equally, clients have a last-minute opportunity to communicate (consciously or unconsciously) anxieties about the weekend ahead or disturbance about anything that may have been said in the Review and/or Community Groups. For this reason, clients are able to opt into the Activities Group at the last minute although, like any other session, they are not allowed to opt out if they have declared the Activities Group to be part of their weekly programme (see 'Attendance expectations', p. 62).

Although the activities session may appear to be less relevant or therapeutic than other more focused groups, it has a vital dual role of providing relaxation and containment for clients as the weekly programme comes to a close. For this reason, it should be given the same care, attention and planning as any other group.

Second stage

Another specially designed component within the model is the evening aftercare programme, which is referred to as Second Stage. Once individuals have stabilized, taken up outside commitments and interests, and reduced to between two and four group sessions per week (in addition to the compulsory Review and Community Groups), they are encouraged to select one of the once- or twice-weekly evening groups which run on Monday to Thursday nights. They attend the evening group of their choice until they feel settled both in the group and with their chosen outside activities such as study or employment. At this time they further reduce attendance and end their day programme commitment having given a minimum of two weeks notice in the Friday review. The movement from full-time day attendance, to part-time attendance, to part-time day attendance *plus* second-stage evening attendance, to second stage only, is phased. The timing of the movement through the process is (within certain limits) determined and controlled by each client within the mechanism of the Friday review. In this way the disruption and trauma so often associated with ending a programme and moving into some form of aftercare is avoided. Clients who make secure attachments to aftercare programmes are known to have a far better prognosis than those who do not (Walker et al. 1983; Rychtarik et al. 1992). This programme structure, which is specifically designed to help clients adjust and settle into aftercare, ensures that a high proportion of those beginning Second Stage manage to continue with their group and hence to continue with working on their abstinence goals.

Although each client will have individual needs and thus a unique pattern to their timetable, typical patterns of attendance will emerge. Most clients begin to cut down their attendance between week three and week five and, if they haven't done so spontaneously, should be strongly encouraged to begin the process by then. The majority reduce significantly (attending three to five sessions per week) between six to ten weeks from when they began. Some then move quickly into a Second Stage group and off the day programme, while others will continue a part-time programme for anything up to six months in conjunction with the gradual development of outside activities. Only then will they feel able to move slowly into the Second Stage programme.

This client-controlled process facilitates the shift away from the highly disruptive treatment/follow-up structure that is such a problematic feature of many of the more traditional methods of intervention. As an alternative model, clients experience attendance in the small, long-term evening group as a continuation of their programme – not as a follow-up to a treatment experience that has been completed. Experience with this programme structure has shown that, once stabilized in work and home settings, the task of weaning off from the evening group begins naturally. Almost all clients will make this shift without major difficulty some time between six and twenty-four months after entering Second Stage.

Both the Review system and the Second Stage structure provide individuals with control, flexibility, and an opportunity of learning from others as well as from their own mistakes. The structures also minimize a major source of potential friction between clients and staff (being forced to attend sessions), which is, in itself, likely to improve outcomes. The PCCP programme is responsive to a range of attachment styles and offers individuals an opportunity to self-regulate and self-medicate with treatment experiences as their stage, mood and need dictate.

To date there have been no randomized controlled trials comparing the effectiveness of the PCCP approach with traditional abstinence-based programmes. It is hoped that this can be rectified as more interest is generated in the model. One team operating the model between November 1995 and October 1997 has gathered two sets of preliminary outcome data internally. This data can be found in Appendix C.

CHAPTER 9
Practical issues

Detoxification

The majority of clients presenting at alcohol advice and treatment services are able to stop drinking on their own without risking medical complications or undue discomfort. Others will not be medically at risk but may experience some unpleasant effects of withdrawal from alcohol, e.g. irritability, sleep disturbance, sweating, etc. A minority will require intensive supervision to monitor for severe withdrawal symptoms such as fitting. If there is any doubt at assessment which category a client is in, a recommendation to seek medical advice must be made. Those individuals requiring (or desiring) medical detoxification can request either a brief inpatient admission or a home detoxification prescription supervised by a family doctor or a member of a community alcohol team. There is no reason for clients to remain in hospital or at home once they are well enough to attend a day programme. The final stages of a detoxification prescription – in most cases a reduced benzodiazapine use – can be monitored from a day centre and should not prevent a client from beginning their day programme treatment.

Creating the culture

The most important model to hold in mind for the appropriate PCCP culture is that of the therapeutic community. The following is a summary (drawn from Kennard 1998b: 19–29) of those key features of standard therapeutic communities that should be replicated within the programme:

- An informal and communal atmosphere (including a flattened hierarchical staff structure)

- A central place for group meetings in the therapeutic programme
- A commitment to sharing the work of maintaining and running the community
- Clients accepting a therapeutic role
- Sharing authority and responsibility (decision-making mechanisms are transparent)
- Sharing certain values and beliefs – for example, that any individual's difficulties are mostly in relation to other people, that therapy is essentially a learning process, that a basic equality exists between all community members – including a psychological equality.

In addition, there must be a shared commitment from all staff to work collectively as a team and to participate in daily handover as well as weekly clinical and business meetings.

The primary differences between a traditional therapeutic community culture and what is required in the PCCP model are:

- The PCCP model is designed for a non-residential setting. As a result the boundaries between inside and outside take on a greater emphasis and often require more direct management from staff (see 'Boundary issues', page 59).
- The Community Group takes place only once a week as compared to the more traditional model of daily community meetings.
- All clients choose when to attend and are not encouraged to attend the full programme after their second week.
- There is more emphasis on the cognitive behavioural therapies and activity-based sessions and less emphasis on the analytic/psycho-dynamic therapies.

In every therapeutic community an emphasis must be placed on creating strong alliances between staff and clients based on warmth, respect and empathy. It is important to remember that, for many clients, it is the alcohol that has been their most reliable and responsive attachment figure (Reading 2002). Clinicians who cannot empathize and articulate the natural ambivalence about a life without substances are not always acting in the client's best interest (Elliott 1987). Motivation is crucial to outcome and will always be enhanced by an environment where clients feel they are being listened to and understood. Wherever possible within the rules of the programme, clients should be given control over how their problems and concerns are defined and how they access help for them.

Counselling

Counselling is an integral part of most treatment programmes regardless of their orientation, and in many services it is the only form in which an intervention is delivered. It is an unusual feature of the PCCP model that counselling is not offered at any time during the programme (see discussion below for distinction between individual meetings and counselling sessions). Various forms of group work are the means by which all therapeutic activity takes place.

With certain kinds of clients, ongoing individual work can create difficulties that group interventions will avoid. For example, the intense therapeutic dependency or attachment will be distributed across the entire staff team and is therefore not as destabilizing for clients during periods of individual staff illness or holiday. It has already been argued that treatment-resistant clients engage in more extreme splitting mechanisms that can result in counsellors becoming first idealized and then denigrated. This in turn lends itself to premature drop out and relapse. Group work facilitates a spread of the 'negative load', and if a particular group leader becomes resented by a particular client, allegiances can be made to other members of the group or to other staff in other groups on the day programme. This increases the likelihood of stability in client attendance and hence in individuals' internal stability. One of the two overall aims of the PCCP model is to contain clients and help them to continue to work on alcohol issues as they define them. Within a group structure and over time, most individuals become stronger and more able to tolerate and deal with feelings of disappointment or resentment towards those around them. In the early months, however, they may feel more comfortable by selecting different groups and different attendance days, thereby avoiding (as opposed to confronting) negative feelings towards another individual. Within the PCCP model this is a completely acceptable strategy and should be encouraged by staff.

Many residential and day care programmes recognize the powerfully curative factors present in group work and so operate a keyworker counselling system within a full group programme. This is not a practice followed on the PCCP model. Experience shows that clients offered this alternative tend to view their weekly counselling session as the time when the meaningful and private therapy takes place (idealization) and the group sessions as less significant, or in some cases insignificant (denigration). The PCCP approach assumes that learning how to relate to and negotiate with peers and authority figures is central to all therapeutic activity. It is the activity which takes place in groups that is primary, not secondary, to the success of the recovery process. For this reason, clients are not encouraged to become distracted from their central task by establishing private, and separate, relationships with individual staff members in ongoing counselling relationships.

While counselling is not part of the PCCP model, there are certain instances when individual meetings are necessary and are integral to the group programme. It is therefore critical for staff to be clear about the distinction between counselling, which is not part of the model, and individual meetings, which are. Individual meetings are offered at certain times for specific purposes and usually last for 20–30 minutes. The following instances might signal the need for an individual meeting:

- Following individual assessment for the programme where further clarification of client aims or programme objectives is needed prior to starting. NB: if more than two individual meetings are required, this may be an indication that a client would be more appropriately steered toward a series of solution-focused counselling sessions rather than the abstinence day treatment programme.
- When clients appear particularly confused, distressed or distracted at any time during their day programme attendance but do not respond adequately to enquiries made during group sessions.
- When clients have undergone sudden outside loss, change or upset, i.e. loss of job, relationship, home, death of family member or anniversary of loss or death. This sometimes may even include the 'loss' of another close client on the programme through relapse.
- When a client seems stuck on the day programme, e.g. undecided about how to cut down, when to move to Second Stage evening group, what activities/work to pick up outside.
- Following the move to Second Stage: for the majority of day clients, the first weeks, and sometimes months, of Second Stage attendance are extremely unsettling and hence a risky time. Although clients are still psychologically held by their part-time day programme with Community Review Structure, and consciously prepared for what to expect from the move, the initiation into Second Stage seems to trigger either feelings of anxiety ('They think I'm better but I'm really not'), or anticlimax/depression ('You mean I've worked this hard and finally gotten into Second Stage and all it is is another group and more talk, talk, talk').

Any of these instances might signal to the staff team that a particular client requires some individual attention. Following the suggestion to meet, it is sometimes the fact that the client feels seen and noticed, rather than the content of the individual meeting itself, which can be the significant stabilizing factor. It is important to bear in mind that individual meetings are *not* counselling sessions. They are *not* intended for deep exploration or to continue beyond one or two meetings, and staff interventions should be determined by these parameters. The primary purpose is to stabilize clients and to help them look at how to move forward with their programme. This may involve bringing their concerns into some of the group sessions of their choice, or may involve avoiding certain individuals or issues by moving on to additional outside interests or changing their programme in some other way. As a general rule, 20–30 minutes is adequate to achieve any of the above aims and one or two meetings are usually sufficient to achieve stabilization. Occasionally, sudden traumatic outside events or a difficult transition to Second Stage may require some additional meetings.

The best way to ensure that individual meetings do not slide into counselling sessions is to keep to time limits and to confine their content to practical problem-solving tasks. If a client brings up a particularly complex or emotional issue, clinicians can use deflecting techniques such as: 'That is such an important insight/part of your history/current issue. I think it is crucial for you to take time to explore this in depth. Can you think of one group in particular (e.g. women's group, general group) which would be a good place to start?' This kind of intervention helps steer the client away from further individual meetings without risking feelings of rejection which can so easily lead to relapse.

Managing boundaries and rules

It is important to respond to boundary and rule infringements as soon as they occur. A client who slides, seemingly unobserved, straight through a boundary will need to test out limits and authority again. There is nothing to be gained by staff discreetly looking the other way even with what seem to be minor issues. It is helpful for a staff team to be clear among themselves and then to communicate to clients the processes by which decisions are taken on the programme (see the discussion above in 'Creating the culture'). It is also important to work towards clarification of those types of issues that are decided:

- Exclusively by clients, e.g. how to collect money and provide adequate supplies of tea and coffee in the client common room, or who is going to chair the business section of the community group.
- By clients and staff together, e.g. whether a meditation session would be useful to introduce into the programme, or whether a series of anger management sessions or sessions on dealing with meeting prospective partners in a drinking environment would be helpful as part of the weekly anxiety management group.

- By staff alone (always after reflecting on conscious and unconscious communications from clients), e.g. a decision to close a client's place on the programme or a decision about staff appointments to the team.

Overall, a lot of attention and discussion is required in order to enable a flattened hierarchy structure to function well. Confusion often exists between a 'no hierarchy' structure, a democracy where staff are somehow elected to represent client views, and a rigid hierarchy where staff take all decisions without any reference to client opinion. One of the first steps in resolving some of the confusion among clients is by enabling the staff team sufficient time and space to clarify some of the confusions amongst themselves.

Rules and guidelines

Each client should be given a copy of the timetable and basic rules and information on the first morning of their day programme attendance. All starters should have two brief meetings with a member of the team to help them work through the written information (Monday a.m. and Thursday p.m. are suggested as ideal times in the first week). It is important to bear in mind that most starters are anxious and will take in very little information from the first introductory meeting. It is therefore important to remind them to re-read the rules and guidelines sections again during their first few weeks to help them to familiarize themselves with the material. The information itself should be as simple as possible and as clear as possible both in language and in content (see Appendix A). Starters should be encouraged to use the Thursday individual meeting to feed back on how they are finding their first week and to raise any questions about rules, guidelines or programme procedures that they are unclear about.

Boundary issues

Working with rules, limits and boundaries is perhaps the single most time-consuming task within the PCCP model. It is particularly relevant because the majority of treatment-resistant clients have few internal boundaries themselves and usually have difficulties with external authority and rules. (These difficulties are just as likely to take the form of never questioning authority figures as always challenging authority figures.) It would not be an exaggeration to say that there are as many potential boundary conflicts as there are problem drinkers and it is certainly not possible to list them all. Suffice it to say that whenever an expectation from staff is present, there will be someone who will test out the expectation to see where the limits are. For this reason alone, a staff team should never ignore boundary issues even if they are not immediately responded to.

In deciding how to respond, a good general rule is to stick to established (written) procedures but to remember that there are exceptions to every rule, which might need to be carefully considered before an intervention is made. In deciding if there is an exception to a broken rule, it is important to explore the relevant issues with the staff team as a whole, and sometimes with the community as a whole, in the community group. Although there are an infinite number of potential boundary conflicts in relation to the guidelines, four major rules need to be highlighted and repeatedly worked through in order to maintain the appropriate therapeutic culture. These four issues, which are discussed in the next section, inevitably come up in various forms as conflicts and require repeated attempts at clarification in settings such as the community group.

The big four rules

Relapse and relapse policy

The details of the relapse policy should be spelled out in the written introductory information but the procedures need to be gone through with clients in the introductory meeting on their first day. If it later becomes clear that a client has not followed the correct procedures as stated in the guidelines (for example, if a client raises in the Monday morning group how glad he or she is to be in because they had a brief 'slip' on Saturday night and felt unsteady afterwards), the group conductor must take action. After congratulating the client on his or her resolve to stop drinking, the group conductor should remind the client, and the rest of the group, of the specific relapse policy which they have agreed to follow. In particular, the policy states that following any drinking incident the client will first phone in and arrange a brief (approximately five minutes) individual meeting with any member of staff in order to explore the circumstances leading to the relapse. The understanding is that this should take place prior to joining the client's first group of the day. When these types of breaches occur, a brief individual meeting should still be arranged to take place as soon as possible after the group, even in cases where the client has worked well on the triggers leading to the slip and how to avoid them in the future. The insistence on arranging a brief meeting represents the commitment to procedures and adherence to procedures around relapse, always a crucial feature for any abstinence-based programme. Despite the fact that most relapsers feel ashamed and embarrassed about 'confessing' a slip to the group, it is almost always the case that fellow group members respond by expressing admiration for the relapser's honesty and commitment to returning to abstinence following the drinking incident. Staff should always be accepting and encouraging, explaining that a relapse can stimulate important learning which, in turn, may promote long-term abstinence.

While representing an acceptance of relapse, it is also crucial for staff to articulate the potential risks and dangers now that a relapse has occurred. While it can be extremely encouraging if individuals stop drinking quickly following a slip and re-state their commitment to abstinence (both verbally and by their presence back on the day programme), this behaviour can also be a dangerous precedent. Clients who pick up a drink or two and then find themselves in a major ongoing binge will quickly learn that they must not pick up even a drink or two if they intend to achieve stability. Clients who pick up a drink or two, have an intense but brief binge and then stop, learn that they can gain control, which enhances self-esteem. But they also learn that when emotional or social pressures feel unmanageable, they can 'break out' for a while and then quickly contain themselves again. Learning that they can engage in this pattern can be extremely dangerous for some individuals as the information will be stored unconsciously and is likely to be tested out again, maybe weeks or even months later. For many clients wishing or needing to choose abstinence as their aim, this process can turn into the beginning of a destructive pattern. For this reason, it is important for staff to represent and articulate both the message of encouragement, support *and* caution following what may seem like a small and nearly insignificant slip.

Of course, the aim of an abstinence-based programme is to enable individuals to abstain and for many clients this will be achieved and maintained. For the remainder, the number of relapses permitted before being asked to leave the programme will be a thought-provoking and time-consuming issue for any staff team. There can be no hard and fast rules for this issue – every client and every circumstance is different. However, some general guidelines for staff are possible to construct:

- It should be rare for a single relapse to result in asking someone to leave the programme. Exceptions might include the following: someone trying to sneak into a group in an intoxicated state; apparent lying about drinking or drug-taking; evidence of bringing alcohol or other drugs into the day centre for personal use or offering them to other clients.
- Following a second reported relapse it is usually time to clarify expectations and limits, i.e. clients need to know that if a third relapse occurs, this indicates that the programme is not helping them to abstain and that they will most likely be asked to give up their place. This leaves some room for exceptional circumstances, while at the same time it tightens the boundary and expectation of abstinence, which can be extremely therapeutic for some individuals.

- Occasionally, a client will smell of alcohol or appear to be under the influence of drugs while in the day centre. In most cases this indicates that they are not able, or do not want, to abstain and probably should have their places closed. In some instances, however, it might be useful to see them individually and then to ask them to go home with a chance to re-start the following day. Sometimes a clear message that lets an individual know that clinicians know and notice, is enough to promote change. A reoccurrence of alcohol odour or intoxicated demeanour must always result in an immediate closure of a place.

No violence or verbal abuse

This rule is certainly the most clear-cut and easy to administer. In order to maintain a culture of therapeutic containment and safety, all clients must know that any incidence of violence will be followed by immediate, non-negotiable close of place with no further offers of readmission. The issue of verbal abuse is a little (but not much) more complex. Often clients are fearful and confused about their own aggression or feelings of hatred and need help differentiating between an expression of anger which is spontaneous, arising from personal pain, and abuse which is far more calculated and controlled and arises directly from the conscious desire to control or do damage to another. These themes and confusions are at the centre of recovery for many clients, and staff will often need to explore the issue in terms of the possibility of healthy, safe expression of feeling, early and often.

Attendance expectations

Attendance is the most frequently abused boundary issue to arise in the practice of the PCCP model and must be handled with great thought and care by staff. All day clients should have been assessed and prepared for starting the day programme before their first day. It is important to explain clearly that before a client is invited to choose an individual part-time programme, that he or she is required to attend all ten group sessions without any exceptions during their first two weeks. Before starting, they are encouraged to think ahead to ensure that they have no commitments which would prevent them attending from Monday to Friday between 11:00 a.m. and 3:00 p.m. (on Thursday from 1:30 to 3:00 p.m. only) for two solid weeks. For the majority of clients, this fairly undemanding commitment presents no problems and they easily get through the first two weeks full-time without difficulty. For others, however, despite a firm commitment being made, phone calls occur with messages of regret and reasons for non-attendance from the early days. Reasons range from illness to late buses to waiting in for an emergency plumber. It is important for staff to receive each communication about absence with expressions of concern and support for the client and sympathetic advice on how to overcome obstacles preventing attendance in the future, e.g. stay warm, have plenty of hot drinks, alternative means of public transport for tomorrow, etc. When the client returns to the programme (in most cases, the next day), it is imperative that they begin to understand that their place on the programme is dependent on their ability to attend every session that they contract into. This of course is set initially at full-time for two weeks and then determined by each client thereafter in the weekly Review Meeting. Clients who constantly test the attendance boundary will never settle into the therapeutic process and, for this reason, 'failure to attend' boundaries should be viewed with nearly the same weight as relapse boundaries. Attending to the boundary is not the same as confrontation and should be experienced as firmly supportive, i.e. 'Maybe our kind of programme is not the ideal one for you. Maybe you would do better on a residential programme or on the kind of day programme where you have to get used to coming in all day every day.' Most clients resent the mere suggestion that they are not mature enough to handle their own timetable and settle down pretty quickly. For the minority who don't, their places should be closed (in some instances, with the possibility of re-assessment) for the sake of the community and the preservation of the culture as a whole.

In instances where new clients fail to attend for any reason during their first two weeks, they should be asked to do an additional week full-time as a matter of course. If by week four or five they are still not managing to attend for two weeks full-time, the indications are that they will not settle into the PCCP programme and they should be offered alternatives early on. There are, of course, clients who are unable to travel regularly to day services due to incarceration or some form of serious illness or disability. Others may be homeless. In these instances, elements of the PCCP model can be incorporated into residential settings, or homeless individuals can be offered 'dry' temporary housing from where they can travel to a day centre.

There are no hard and fast guidelines about the type or length of programme a particular individual should choose. The point of the PCCP model is that each client is unique and will make personal choices about what kinds of interventions (more cognitive, more activity-based, more psychodynamic) are best for their aptitudes and interests and stage of recovery. They will also make personal choices about how intense a programme they need, how much they are ready to take on outside activities, which clients and staff they like working with, and which they would rather avoid. Some of the choices they make will be mistakes. For example, a premature or rapid reduction of attendance might lead directly to a relapse. It is inherent, however, in the PCCP approach that it is sometimes the wrong personal choice in the right environment that can result in the most important and meaningful learning experiences. Clients are encouraged to talk to one another before making choices, and above all to learn from their mistakes. This includes converting their experiences (mistakes and all) into future decision-making. The role of staff in this exercise is to witness and record the personal choices of clients, to offer feedback, encouragement or words of warning as feels appropriate, and then to back clients in the choices they make. Above all, staff must always represent and defend the client's right to choose. Clients will gradually begin to experience the full weight of responsibility for the personal choices they make. Staff should support and reflect the emphasis on responsibility by expecting clients to keep to their commitments with regard to the programme and by taking action if clients repeatedly do not.

No socializing or outside contact

It is important to discuss and clarify why this rule is in place and is taken so seriously. The discussion needs to take place at regular intervals in the Community Group partly because the rule is counter-intuitive to what most clients think will be helpful and partly because it runs contrary to that of many alcohol agencies and associations such as Alcoholics Anonymous. It is important for staff to be alert and sensitive to any indications that outside socializing is taking place, e.g. clients leaving or arriving together, having outside information such as what someone else's house looks like or what they had for dinner last night. When raising the rule about no outside contact, it is a good idea to articulate the fact that, like some drinking incidences, it is impossible for staff to police or know if the rule has been infringed: 'We know that we can't know what you do and with whom you do it, when you aren't here.' Nonetheless, clients should be clear that if staff learn about outside contact (via direct observation or information from another client) the offending individuals will most likely be asked to leave the programme. This information usually comes as a surprise to clients but elicits the appropriate degree of seriousness about infringement of the rule. They will understand that they can most likely get away with this form of rule-breaking but if they are spotted there will be no possibility of extenuating circumstances. This is all most clients need to know in order to stay away from fellow clients when outside the building. It is always a good idea, however, to offer the reasons why the rule is in place, for community discussion:

- It avoids subgroups and 'secrets' among the community group.
- It avoids relapse in one triggering relapse in another.
- It avoids the possibility of a client/friend becoming a nuisance on the telephone or at home. There are no possible implications for outside life regardless of what is said in groups.

- It ensures a greater degree of confidentiality and therapeutic intensity during group sessions because everything takes place in the groups and is shared.
- Fellow clients are like working colleagues. The programme does not aim to provide friends or lovers for clients. It does seek to enable clients to practise new skills and then to go out and make new relationships and friendships. Once clients reach Second Stage and are off the day programme they are free to socialize with any other clients as long as they are not in the same Second Stage group.

Most clients have never thought of the possible complications that can arise from meeting outside, and usually express relief at hearing that no matter how close they feel to some individuals on the programme, everything is left inside the groups and never carried into outside life. Those individuals who do run into each other at other clinics or AA meetings can soon learn how to greet but not engage with fellow day-programmers.

Staffing

With the exception of groups such as music appreciation, art class or yoga, which are run by specialist sessional workers, the PCCP programme should be run by full-time or nearly full-time clinicians only. The Day Programme caters for a maximum of 24 clients and the Second Stage programme caters for a maximum of five groups with up to seven clients in each, and together this requires a minimal staffing of three and a half to four clinical posts. Administration and reception staff should be factored in to any staffing budget over and above the clinical team. Although it is possible to offer some flexibility along the full-time/part-time continuum, most of the team should be full-time, and those who are not should work a minimum of 21 hours over four days. Breaking posts down into part-time sessional workers is not effective when operating the PCCP model as the core team needs to be in regular daily contact. This is essential in order to keep a continuity of client preoccupations across sessions. It also helps the team contain and make use of any splitting that individual clients are engaged in, between groups or between staff.

Funding and monitoring of clients in the UK

Most clients in both voluntary and statutory sectors need to secure funding in order to attend substance misuse programmes. Historically, residential and day programmes have been costed as a whole and a charge made for the total treatment programme, e.g. six weeks' or four months' attendance. This is not the most sensible approach to costing the PCCP programme since it does not take account of the wide range of individual differences. It does not seem fair to charge funders the same for one client who completes the day programme in seven weeks, cutting down to five sessions a week in week four, and another client who attends for six months, managing to reduce their attendance significantly only by week 12. A more practical approach is to cost the full-time weekly programme (ten groups) and then simply to invoice funders at the end of the month for the number of groups the client has contracted into in each weekly review. This not only provides a meaningful costing but also provides funders with a good ongoing sense of each client's progress and movement through the programme. Invoicing is a simple procedure that can be done at regular intervals on the basis of the weekly review notes kept in each client's file.

While some clients are self-funding and have no links to outside professional bodies, others will be subject to ongoing monitoring by social workers, probation officers and other professionals involved with Integrated Care Programmes (ICPs). Monthly or bi-monthly three-way meetings can easily be arranged with relevant outside professionals, where clients can refer to their weekly review notes as indicators of problems and movement through their programme. One core team member should always attend the first part of these meetings in order to address concerns or questions from those less familiar with the PCCP approach and to consolidate professional links. Most clients are then happy to spend the bulk of their meeting alone with outside professionals.

'But we already do that!'

There will undoubtedly be some clinicians who have read the description of the PCCP model and feel that they have been practising this approach, more or less, for years. It is true that the model does allow for considerable flexibility. The day programme can be altered both in terms of content, and in average expected attendance rates, to make it more responsive to a wide range of substance misusers or dual diagnosis clients. However, there are certain practices and principles that must be rigidly adhered to if the model is to function effectively.

- There should be no more than ten groups of a wide diversity and intensity in the weekly programme.
- All staff must be full-time (with the exception of teachers in sessions such as yoga or art) and meet daily.

- Individual counselling should not be made available to those on the day programme.
- Review and Community Groups should take place on a Friday morning where all full-time staff and all day clients are present.
- Within a containing, supportive therapeutic community culture, all clients should be encouraged to reduce day programme attendance and take up outside activities as quickly as is safely possible for them to do so.

CHAPTER 10

Final thoughts

The preceding pages outline the major principles, aims and structures inherent in the PCCP model. With adequate training and supervision, it should be possible for an alcohol team with some psychodynamic understanding to establish the programme in a day centre setting. Individual clinical styles and techniques are always important matters and these have not been explored here. Further study of some of the writings by any of the experienced substance misuse practitioners cited in the text is highly recommended.

Traditional group psychotherapy technique does have a role in the PCCP model but, as most experts suggest, certain differences should be borne in mind. Substance misuse clinicians must always be ready to take an educative and directive stance at certain times in their day-to-day practice. There is often a need to work actively to reduce tension, anxiety or conflict between members in groups. Psychotherapy with this group of individuals must maintain its emphasis on being supportive rather than interpretative (Kernberg et al. 1989). At all times, clinical interventions should be designed to make it more likely that clients will continue with treatment – an aim to be borne in mind from the first two weeks of full-time attendance to the final fortnight in Second Stage.

Deciding when and how to make interventions in the service of this aim is always a fine clinical judgement. It is certainly important to remember that, in the early phases, clients have very little 'psychic muscle' (Elliott 1987) with which to cope with discomfort. By the time they reach Second Stage, they should be more resilient. However, without the freedom to move away from individuals who provoke difficult feelings – a freedom that is inherent in the day programme structure – great care still needs to be taken in enabling clients to maintain their attachment to the treatment setting.

One way to further promote a helpful attachment to therapy is by assisting clients to take up new activities and resources in the wider community. Recovery is not only about what happens in the therapeutic environment but also what happens outside it. Many clients are not experienced in making community links and need the support and help of interested and knowledgeable staff. Potential links include adult education, sports or arts activities, voluntary work as well as outside advice and support networks. In this respect Alcoholics Anonymous, while not acceptable to everyone as a recovery programme, is a good way to access additional resources as well as social contacts, and should be encouraged in those who are willing to try. Most of these kinds of outside links can enhance a client's sense of self-esteem and enjoyment of life, all of which contributes to motivation in continuing with therapy and recovery. If individuals can be helped to carry on in treatment as a priority, then they will continue to make creative use of the programme as a whole and then in parts as the other areas of life grow and evolve. In learning to maintain attachments over time, clients are gradually able to develop and master their own interpersonal skills. These are the very skills necessary to developing a fulfilling life, free from substance misuse and dependence.

Alcohol-related statistics

Statistics relating to alcohol consumption and health in the UK

- The number of deaths from alcohol-related diseases increased by 38% between 1992 and 1997 (DOH 1999).
- The number of deaths where alcohol is a factor is estimated at between 25,000 and 40,000 a year (Royal College of Physicians 1987).
- One in six Accident and Emergency admissions are alcohol-related, rising to eight out of 10 during peak times, such as Friday and Saturday nights (Pirmohamed and Gilmore 2000; HEA 1998).
- 20–30% of all accidents are connected to heavy drinking (Alcohol Concern 2002a).
- In one 12-month period, there were 72,500 hospital admissions with mental and behavioural disorders due to alcohol (DOH 1999).
- 65% of suicide attempts are linked with excessive drinking (DOH 1993).

Statistics relating to alcohol consumption and crime in the UK

The relationship between alcohol consumption and crime is a complex one. While it cannot be argued that alcohol directly causes crime, it is a contributing factor in many cases. In instances of:

- 65% of homicides
- 75% of stabbings
- 70% of beatings
- 50% of domestic assaults

the offender has been drinking (British Medical Association; see also Alcohol Concern 2001).

Statistics relating to alcohol consumption and health in the USA

- An estimated 110,000 lives are lost annually due to alcohol-related problems (USDHHS 2000).
- More than two million Americans currently suffer from alcohol-related liver disease (NIAAA 1998a).
- 25% of all general hospital admissions are related to alcohol misuse (Join Together 1998).
- 78% of alcohol-dependent men and 86% of alcohol-dependent women have suffered from some other psychiatric disorder at some time in their life (Anthony et al. 1994). Mental disorders of all types, including affective and anxiety disorders, occur more frequently among alcohol abusers (Kessler 1996).
- 38% of deaths due to traffic accidents were alcohol-related. Between 1 a.m. and 6 a.m. on weekday mornings, one in seven drivers are drunk (NHTSA 1999).

Statistics relating to alcohol and crime in the USA

The relationship between alcohol and crime is a complex one. While it cannot be argued that alcohol directly causes crime, it is a contributing factor in many cases. In instances of:

- 86% of homicides
- 37% of assaults
- 60% of sexual offences
- 57% of male marital violence
- 27% of female marital violence
- 13% of child abuse offences

the offender has been drinking (Roizen 1997).
  In addition:

- 41% of those on probation
- 41% of those in local jails
- 38% of those in state prisons

reported that they had been drinking when committing their offences (Greenfeld 1998).

Handouts from ACCEPT

The following handouts were produced by ACCEPT (Alcohol Community Centres for Prevention and Treatment) which offered day treatment to problem drinkers for over 25 years and practised the PCCP model from 1995 to 1999. They provide an excellent template for the kind of information PCCP clients should be given. 'Client Guidelines' can be worked through with all new starters, individually or in small groups, as part of their first week induction process. Clients should then be reminded and encouraged to refer to the document throughout their stay. The 'Second Stage Guidelines' should be given to clients at least two weeks before they attend their first Second Stage aftercare session.

ACCEPT: Client guidelines for daytime programme

The purpose of these guidelines is to help make your time at ACCEPT as positive and effective as possible.

Confidentiality

ACCEPT is committed to maintaining your privacy and the confidentiality of what you express here. You are also responsible for supporting other clients' confidentiality. Issues raised in groups should not be brought into the coffee room or taken out of ACCEPT. We would ask you, therefore, to please respect other clients' privacy.

Staff at ACCEPT do share information about clients but names and identifiable personal details never go outside of the organization without your clear written permission. This includes partners and relatives who may ask for information about you.

We would make exceptions to the confidentiality rule only if we felt that your life or the life of some other person was at risk.

If you have contact with other professionals involved in your recovery process (such as psychiatrists, psychotherapists, counsellors, welfare

73

officers, social workers, probation officers, keyworkers, etc.), we may need to be in liaison with them. If you are in contact with other professionals, would you please ensure you inform a member of staff in your first week, if you have not already done so. We shall ask for written permission for ACCEPT to be in liaison with them. We shall not make contact with them without your permission.

In addition, *if* you continue to receive ongoing therapy externally, we would ask you to bring any insights you gain into groups at ACCEPT.

Attendance

Your first two weeks – it is important that you attend the programme every day in your first two weeks in order to give you the opportunity to try all the groups on the programme and to provide you with a sufficient level of stability and support, which is an important aspect of the therapy process.

If you are unable to complete the first two weeks, for whatever reason, you will be asked to complete another one or two full weeks before choosing your programme options.

After your initial two weeks, you will have the opportunity of selecting your programme on a weekly basis at the Client Review Meeting. At this meeting you will be able to talk about your progress and get some feedback from other clients and staff. You will also be asked to choose your programme and a personal focus which will form the basis of your contract to yourself for that week. It is important that you attend the programme on the days you have chosen. (See under Clients Review for more information.)

You will be expected on the programme on the days you have contracted to attend, and on these days only. However, should it transpire that something you have planned outside ACCEPT falls through and you are feeling vulnerable, you are encouraged to phone in and one of the staff will talk through with you what you might do with your time on that day.

If, for some reason, you definitely cannot come in on a day when you have contracted to, make sure you phone and tell us. If you are absent due to sickness, please phone in every day to maintain contact.

You are encouraged to arrive early for the groups as it is important for your therapy that you are there when the groups start. There is a maximum of 15 minutes leeway when latecomers will be permitted to join the group. However, it is the group's responsibility to challenge individuals on frequent lateness. The implications for you and for the community will be explored in groups.

The exception to the 15 minutes leeway is the Review Meeting when you may join the group at any point if you are late.

Planning sessions are available on a one-to-one basis with a core team member. These sessions are a useful means of reviewing your development in terms of your use of the programme and life outside. They can also be used if you are undecided about which groups to attend, how much and when to cut down your programme, and if you are considering leaving the programme and/or going on to a Second Stage group.

Groups

- Groups are what you make of them – try to tell people what you think and feel. There will always be a member of staff present if you need extra support outside group time.
- Do not be concerned if it takes a while to feel confident about contributing to groups – there is no obligation to perform.
- There is no consuming of food and drink and no smoking during group sessions.

It seems natural to want to extend the friendships made at ACCEPT to outside life. However, socializing leads to complications and problems. Do not put your therapy at risk by offering your address or telephone number or by having any outside contact with other clients while at ACCEPT. Clients who do not adhere to this may be asked to leave the programme.

Clients Review

Every Friday morning at 10.15 a.m. all the clients and core staff meet together to review the progress of each client. In your first week you just say a bit about how your week has been, but from your second week onwards you have a chance to:

(a) talk about how the week has been, highlighting any significant events or insights and to say how you have been feeling during the week
(b) receive feedback from other clients and staff. This might include how they have experienced you this week or it could be some advice or guidance they would like to pass on to you
(c) choose your programme for the following week
(d) choose a focus for the following week. The focus may be something very practical like seeing your doctor, going for a swim or to an AA meeting. Alternatively, you may decide you want to focus on something internally which has come up in groups, like exploring your childhood or expressing your anger in a more contained way, or being assertive with someone close to you.

The Review Meeting differs from most other groups and it is not a therapy group. When others are giving you feedback, you do not have the opportunity of responding. You are asked simply to listen to what others have to say to you and reflect on it. If you wish to respond to what someone has said to you, then you have the opportunity to do so in the Community Group which follows the Review Meeting.

The Community Group

The Community Group meets following a short break after the Clients Review. It is an opportunity for all clients and staff to be together and to discuss any issue that affects the ACCEPT community – either to do with the building, the facilities or the groups. It is also an opportunity to express any thoughts or feelings about the Clients Review.

Art and Yoga Classes

The Art and Yoga groups run on Wednesday mornings. New clients are strongly encouraged to attend one of them on a regular basis, say for six weeks. It is quite difficult to get a good feel for these two groups by going once or twice. Many clients experience the benefit of attending these groups only after they have been a few times.

Meditation

There is a weekly Meditation between 3.30 and 4.00 p.m. on Wednesdays. This is optional; you are not required to contract to attend.
    It is facilitated and is an opportunity to meditate with other clients.

Dream Workshop

This is an optional session, facilitated monthly on Mondays 3.30–4.30 p.m. You don't need to have a dream in mind in order to attend. There will be the opportunity to learn techniques for exploring dreams, and to exchange ideas about other people's dreams in a relaxed way in the session.

Special Groups

From time to time, clients express a desire for a 'special' group to focus on a specific issue. Often these are quite sensitive topics and may include, for example, sexuality. If you would like us to run a group on a particular topic that interests you, please feel free to ask. You may, if you prefer, put forward an idea anonymously through the Suggestions Box. These groups, like the Dream Workshop, are held outside the main programme at a time and date of which you will be informed.

Alcohol and Drug Use

Alcohol substitutes

You are asked not to drink Kaliber, Iceberg or other alcohol substitutes. Using such substitutes is a way of holding on to the illusion (and habit) of drinking, and can lead to a relapse.

Mood-altering substances

The use of any mood-altering substances (including cannabis) blocks progress in therapy. Do not swap one dependence for another. Clients who continue to use mood altering substances will be asked to leave the programme.

Prescription drugs

If you are considering making a change in your use of prescribed drugs – either reducing, stopping altogether or starting a course of medication – please let a member of ACCEPT staff know what you are planning to do, and make changes only after consulting your doctor.

Relapse

It is important to voice your doubts and fears if you feel like a drink. Ask for help sooner rather then later. There will always be someone to talk to you.

If you do have a relapse, no matter how small, please contact us by telephone as soon as possible. It is important that you speak to a member of staff in person before going back into the programme.

ACCEPT is an alcohol-free building. Please do not turn up intoxicated.

It is very important that if you know that another client is drinking, you talk it over with a member of staff. This is not being disloyal to the other client – it is more disloyal to indulge or condone their drinking. This is harmful, not only to their recovery but yours as well. Talk it over with a member of staff if you are concerned.

Ending The Daytime Programme

Your attendance on the Daytime Programme is not timelimited. The minimum duration of time that you are required to stay is the first two full-time weeks. How long you stay on the programme beyond that will depend on a number of factors, including work and family commitments and how safe you feel in terms of maintaining your abstinence.

While you are here and when you feel ready, you are encouraged to build up a variety of outside activities, which may include:

- part-time or full-time paid work
- voluntary work
- attending college (either retraining or a course for interest)
- exercise! – sport
- attendance at AA/SOS meetings
- hobbies and pastimes.

In our experience, those clients who *slowly* cut down their programme (having spent, as a guide, perhaps the first 4–6 weeks on a full time basis), while building up a positive alcohol-free lifestyle outside, are more likely to be successful in achieving ongoing abstinence. Also, it is at the stage when there is a balance between attendance here (as a guide, 3–4 groups per week, including Friday morning) and activities outside that a client feels ready to leave the Day Time Programme. This process varies in duration from person to person. You can book an individual session to discuss your progress including your plans for leaving.

Clients sometimes experience difficulties in deciding when to leave. This may happen quite naturally if you feel safe here and feel you have benefited from the programme. However, there is a natural inclination to hang on to the programme and to fear what will happen without the support of the other clients and the groups. You are encouraged to talk about your feelings about ending your day programme in order to help with the transition.

This is an opportunity to experience endings positively and can therefore be an invaluable learning experience.

Second Stage groups are available for those planning to leave the Daytime Programme. These currently run once or twice weekly in the evenings (times vary) between Monday and Thursday.

If you join a Second Stage group you can have an overlap with the Daytime Programme of up to 10 weeks. We recommend at least a 4-week overlap.

Second Stage Guidelines can be obtained from the office, or speak to a member of staff if you are interested in joining one.

Building

The coffee room is your area. Please keep it clean and tidy – a pleasant place to be in.

Smoking Policy – ACCEPT operates a non-smoking policy throughout most of its premises. Clients may smoke in the coffee room except when a group is in progress.

Use of other rooms – if you prefer a non-smoking environment, other rooms are available as a quiet space when one-to-one or groups are not in progress.

Equal Opportunities

ACCEPT has a statement of Anti-Discriminatory Practice. (See Attached). We ask you to consider your language and behaviour in the building and within groups in the light of this.

If it comes to your attention that someone you know is wishing to join the Day Programme then please raise this with a member of staff as soon as possible. We shall talk to you about the nature of the relationship and any concerns you may have about confidentiality before any decisions are made.

ACCEPT: Client guidelines for Second Stage groups

These guidelines are intended to assist clients considering joining Second Stage groups.

Joining

If you are attending ACCEPT's daytime programme, it is expected that before joining a Second Stage group, you will have cut down on your full-time programme to a point where you feel comfortable and stable attending on a part-time basis, with an outside structure which supports you. Ideally, you will still be attending two daytime groups per week plus the Review Meeting and Community Group before joining Second Stage.

If you are attending more than four daytime groups (including the Review Meeting and Community Group), it is unlikely that you are ready to join Second Stage.

When you have started to cut back your daytime programme to a comfortable level and you are thinking about Second Stage, you should discuss this with a member of the core team or bring it into one of the daytime groups for discussion.

Choosing

In deciding which Second Stage group to join, you might like to consider the following factors:

- Do you want a once or twice weekly group?
- Which days of the week can you attend, given your commitments?
- Which facilitator do you feel most comfortable or uncomfortable with?

Choosing a group based on your level of comfort with the facilitator may not necessarily be the best option. There may be some constructive thera-peutic learning involved in working in a group where there is a member of staff about whom you have difficult feelings. Alternatively, a facilitator may hold certain qualities which you think you would find beneficial in your therapy. The same principle applies to choosing a group based on the other members. Negative feelings may be useful to work through in the group.

When you are thinking about joining a Second Stage group, you should talk it through with a member of staff and then speak to the facilitator of the group you wish to join. The facilitator must give the other group members two weeks' notice of a new member joining and will agree your date of joining with you.

Payment of fees

When your place in the group has been agreed, you should arrange to see the Administrator regarding payments. ACCEPT offers a fee structure based on a sliding scale depending upon income, as follows:

Unemployed or low paid	£2.00 per session.
Income over £10 000 p.a.	£5.00 per session.
Income over £15 000 p.a.	£10.00 per session.
Income over £20 000 p.a.	£15.00 per session.
Income over £30 000 p.a.	£20.00 per session.

There is a bursary system available for a limited period of time for cases of real need. Other financial circumstances will be taken into account.

Fees are payable before the start of the group each evening. Please pay in the office. Cheques will be accepted over £5.00.

You will be charged for *all* sessions once you are a member of a group, including those from which you are absent. You will not be charged if the group does not take place. The fee is payable for groups that are self-facili-tated and for groups that run for only an hour if there are fewer than three clients in attendance.

In the case of unplanned leaving where the group member con-cerned has not given an ending date, the Group Facilitator will write to invite her/him in for a talk about what's happening in the group and/or offer a one-to-one session. If there is no response to this, after a few weeks the place will be closed and an invoice will be sent for any unpaid sessions.

Overlap of Second Stage group and daytime programme

Once you have joined a Second Stage group, it is expected that you will start planning to cut back further on the day programme with a view to leaving the day programme altogether. There is no time-frame to the overlap of day programme and Second Stage group. However, it is expected that an average will be four to ten weeks. Individual circumstances will always be taken into account.

Membership

Membership of the Second Stage group is not time limited, although it is expected that members are likely to stay in the group for up to two years or more.

It is important that you let your group know in advance if you are unable to attend a session for any reason. Your well-being will be of concern to both your facilitator and other group members. You can always leave a message for your group with the office.

The telephone number is: _____.

Please let your group have at least a week's notice of any planned absences. Your facilitator will give you adequate notice of his or her planned absences. In the event of sickness on the part of the facilitator, ACCEPT will contact you if the group is not running. It is, therefore, important to keep the office updated with your address and contact telephone number, particularly for the day of the week that your group runs.

The maximum group membership will be seven. The group will be given two weeks notice of new members joining.

Timekeeping

You will be informed of the start time of your group (these are variable depending upon which group you join).

Clients are advised to arrive between 10 and 30 minutes before the start of the group to avoid lateness as the group will start on time. Your facilitator will let you know what arrangements there are (if any) for latecomers.

Confidentiality

ACCEPT is committed to maintaining your privacy and the confidentiality of what you express here. You are also responsible for supporting other group members' confidentiality. It is important that group members respect each other's privacy.

Staff at ACCEPT do share information about clients, but names and identifiable personal details never go outside of the organization without your clear written permission. This includes partners and relatives who may ask for information about you.

Liaison with professionals

In addition, if you have any contact with other professionals involved in your recovery process, (such as psychiatrists, psychotherapists, counsellors, welfare officers, social workers, probation officers or keyworkers) we may need to be in liaison with them.

If you are in contact with other professionals, please ensure that you inform your group facilitator *if* you have not already informed the office. We shall ask for written permission for ACCEPT to be in liaison with them.

We shall not make contact with them without your permission.

Participation in groups

Groups are what you make them – don't be frightened to tell people what you think and feel.

Should you ever feel in need of extra support because of a crisis or uncertainty, bring it to the group immediately.

If you need extra support, ring to book a one-to-one meeting with your facilitator.

Socializing with other clients

It seems natural to want to extend the friendships made at ACCEPT to outside life. However, socializing leads to complications and problems. Don't put your therapy at risk by offering your address or telephone number or by having any outside contact with other clients with whom you are in therapy whilst at ACCEPT.

Clients who do not adhere to this may be asked to leave their group.

Relapse

It is important to voice your doubts and fears if you feel like having a drink. Ask for help sooner rather then later. There will always be someone to talk to you.

If you do have a relapse, no matter how small, please bring it to the group immediately. If you need extra support, ring in to book an individual meeting with your group facilitator.

ACCEPT is an alcohol-free building. Please do not turn up intoxicated.

Early days at ACCEPT: a guide to developing a positive non-drinking lifestyle

The first few days

After you have stopped drinking, you may find yourself depressed, confused and possibly touched by feelings of despair, guilt, anxiety, anger and resentments. These are normal withdrawal symptoms and are commonly experienced.

You may, at first, find it difficult to sleep. Do not worry. Lack of sleep never killed anyone. Alcohol and drugs can. Take long walks. Drink hot milk mixed with honey before going to bed. Keep books and magazines at your bedside.

No matter what, do not permit any build-up of feelings to trap you into picking up that first drink. Continued abstinence is the key to treatment and recovery .

Other problems (domestic, financial and legal), no matter how pressing, are best dealt with from a foundation of abstinence. Drinking more alcohol will only make matters worse.

Consult ACCEPT staff who may assist you in dealing with your problems.

Essential to relax and eat well

Keep in mind that the world is probably not coming to an end today and you will survive. So *relax*. Put the past and future aside and concentrate your energies on getting through today as comfortably as you can. Try to eat often. Plenty of protein: eggs, fish, milk, wheatbread, etc. As time goes by your appetite will improve. Drink lots of liquids but not too much coffee. Caffeine may increase tension, nervousness and sleeplessness. Unless you are a diabetic, take as much sugar as you can in the early days.

Take a sweet instead of a drink

If you do feel nervous, anxious or depressed, eat sweets, a bar of chocolate or get a packet of glucose tablets (Dextrosol) from your chemist. It is far better to eat a sweet rather than pick up that first drink.

If you are diabetic, consult your doctor and follow his recommendations now that you have stopped drinking.

Healthy eating habits

We advise extra sugar and sweets in the short term only, until you are well stabilized in abstinence and new, positive habit-patterns have started to take hold. Eventually, it is best to establish a healthy eating pattern based upon sound principles of nutrition.

Don't worry about gaining weight now; your weight will probably adjust itself as time passes. Bear in mind that by stopping drinking you have already reduced your calorie intake dramatically.

Reliability

Establish daily performance and reliability. If you can't attend ACCEPT or keep an individual appointment make a phone call and let us know how you are.

Drinking stories

Be aware of the dangers of recounting and swapping 'drinking stories'. These are an indication of a continuing obsession with the past and with drink, and a way of hiding from yourself and your present feelings. In addition they can be very boring for others.

Here and now

The emphasis here is not on past mistakes, but on the *here and now*. Concentrate on identifying self-destructive habit-patterns and making positive changes. Work on gaining new insights, new strengths and developing survival skills.

Involvement with clients

While meeting and sharing with other people who have had similar problems is one of the chief therapeutic assets of ACCEPT, any emotional involvement with another client tends to be a diversion from your own recovery: it can lead to you channelling all your energy into one person, resulting in all sorts of disastrous situations.

The idea is not for you to form dependencies on the clients or staff here, but to develop the skills to make positive emotional ties outside. Avoid lending money or exchanging addresses and telephone numbers, as this can lead to unpleasant situations.

What happens at ACCEPT?

The first few days here will probably feel very confusing, like any new experience. It is important, however, for you to maintain a routine and meet commitments, as this is part of the process of recovery. Make sure you arrive here at 10.00 a.m., and treat the programme as your Number One Daily Priority in life.

Many people feel guilty at first because they actually enjoy coming here; there is nothing wrong with enjoying the good feeling that beginning to tackle your problems gives you.

Your personal programme

After two weeks of attending fulltime, you will choose your programme at the Weekly Review Meeting; you may wish to attend a few specific sessions a week, as opposed to attending fulltime.

This will give you the opportunity to work out a schedule specifically tailored to your individual needs. Study and re-study the ACCEPT programme.

The meaning of groups

A variety of groups, ranging from Creative Group Therapy, Relapse Prevention and Acting for Change to Growing Through Loss and Clients Review are the main therapeutic resources at ACCEPT. You may find them strange at first, since it is rare in ordinary society to have the opportunity to talk honestly about whatever is troubling you. Study the Group Experience Questionnaire and learn from it.

If you are shy, it may be some time before you find the courage to talk. This does not matter at all, since every individual must travel at his or her own pace. Listen and learn is a good policy for some.

There is no obligation to perform or entertain. There may be silences in some of the groups, but these should not be a cause for anxiety; it is up to each group member to get what he/she can out of a group, and there is no need to talk for the sake of talking.

General information

Staff are available for private talks. Group meetings are held every day except Saturday and Sunday. Study your schedule. If you feel 'edgy' or 'blue', don't just sit about feeling sorry for yourself – get involved.

We can help you

Use ACCEPT to help you develop a new, healthy behaviour pattern, new survival skills and generally organize your life along more productive, comfortable ways.

Avoid hasty decisions

Try not to act hastily or make long-term decisions (such as returning to work) until you are ready to do so. Talk over your plans and problems in the group. Think twice, three times before acting. Impulsiveness can be dangerous.

Keystones of recovery

Desire to succeed combined with continuity and reliability are the keystones of recovery. Establish a plan for attendance and treatment and adhere to it. See your GP or psychiatrist regularly. Do not permit changing priorities to divert you from your personal programme.

Ground rules about not drinking

You are not permitted to attend ACCEPT if you have been drinking during the past 24 hours. It is absolutely essential to concentrate your mind on avoiding picking up that first drink. If necessary, break the day down into four-hour sections during which you concentrate on not drinking. If you have the urge to drink, think of an alternative strategy such as making a phone call, taking a hot bath, eating something sweet, etc. The urge will pass.

Halt syndrome

As time goes on and as you learn new coping skills, positive non-drinking will become an ordinary fact of life. However, at all times be aware of the HALT syndrome. Halt stands for:

HUNGRY   ANGRY   LONELY   TIRED

Avoid getting into any situation where the combination of these dangerous states takes over from your good judgement.

In case of trouble

If things go wrong and you do relapse, do not become hysterical and keep on drinking. Stop drinking as soon as you can and telephone ACCEPT. Arrange to come in and have a talk with one of the staff before you rejoin the programme. Alternatively, see your GP.

Almost all relapses can be traced back to one or two weeks before you actually pick up that first drink. Try to use the relapse as a 'learning experience' so that you will be that much stronger in the future.

Other clients

If, by any chance, you become aware that another client is finding it impossible to abstain, please discuss this with your fellow clients and with the staff. Remember that you are doing no favours by allowing others to drink or by covering up for them – you are encouraging their dependence by remaining silent and you might be 'helping' them to destroy themselves. By not confronting the situation you may jeopardize your own and others' recovery.

Impulsiveness and impatience

Two of the greatest personality problems interfering with stable long-term recovery are impulsiveness and impatience.

Impatience to leave ACCEPT, combined with fear of becoming over-dependent upon the Centre, may lead you to decide to discontinue your programme of recovery before you are ready.

You probably have many years of potentially healthy living before you, so it is important that you put your impatient desires in perspective. Another one, two or even three months in a treatment programme are very small periods of time when compared to the years of life ahead of you.

So why not organize a successful and lasting recovery in the Here and Now while you are at ACCEPT? Discuss this with your fellow clients and with the staff. Take all the time you need and build a solid foundation of recovery and effective living skills before you think of leaving.

Dependence

Our long experience has proved that people do not get dependent upon ACCEPT in the long term. It is perfectly OK to be dependent upon the Centre in the short term, and as your recovery progresses, you will automatically find yourself developing a degree of self-sufficiency and independence that you probably never experienced before. The 'bottom line' is that even if you wished to become dependent upon ACCEPT we would not permit this to happen.

Non-smoking rooms

We ask you not to smoke in the group or counselling rooms, both for the benefit of those who do not smoke and for your own recovery. For those of you who wish to smoke, the coffee lounge is available during each break.

Avoid drinking situations

Dependent drinkers may be said to be obsessed with the idea of alcohol. Accordingly, they often think that everyone else drinks and when they stop drinking may feel that their new behaviour is abnormal – that they are outcasts from society.

This is simply and categorically not so.

There are many millions of people who choose not to drink alcohol beverages for a variety of reasons, e.g. health, religion, don't like the taste, don't like the effect, and so forth.

Therefore, when you begin abstinence, you are neither alone nor unusual.

During your drinking career you may have consciously or unconsciously sought out the company of other drinkers and drinking situations. Some people reach the unhappy stage in life where their sole leisure activity is drinking in pubs with pub acquaintances, or at home alone.

New habit patterns

Whatever your past drinking pattern, it is strongly recommended that in the early months of abstinence you alter your habit patterns drastically (including those at home) and avoid drinking situations as much as possible.

Unhealthy drinking environment

The reasons are threefold. First, the drinking atmosphere found in pubs, at parties, etc., is not conductive to healthy recovery. Even though, in these drinking situations, you feel positive about your abstinence and refuse alcohol with confidence, this close association with alcohol may lead to keeping the drinking obsession alive in both your conscious and subconscious mind, thereby causing subsequent feelings (within days or weeks) of discomfort, or even craving for alcohol.

Second, by not changing your old habit patterns you are denying yourself the opportunities to develop new, healthy activities and alternative uses of leisure time. You will diminish your chances for making definite, productive and rewarding changes in your lifestyle.

Third, the very proximity of alcohol in drinking situations during the first few months puts you at great risk, sooner or later, of picking up that first drink in an unguarded moment.

New interests

Experience suggests that those who develop new interests and regular leisure activities make the most effective recoveries.

How do I become a comfortable, positive non-drinker?

During recovery, you will probably be drawn into, or be unable to avoid, certain drinking situations. It is important, therefore, that you develop, and even rehearse with fellow recoverers, or in front of a mirror, or in interaction groups, your positive responses when invited to have a drink.
Some effective responses may take the following forms:

'I'd like ginger ale.'
'No thanks. I'd prefer plain tonic water' (or whatever).
'No thanks, I don't drink.'
'Doctor's orders, absolutely no alcohol.'
'I'm on a diet. I'll have a slimline tonic.'
'If you don't mind. I'll take a soft drink. Alcohol just does not agree with me.'

Express yourself in a clear, positive tone. Do not hesitate or waffle. Your life may depend upon it.

Soft drinks at parties

If you attend a party, get a soft drink in to your hand as quickly as possible. As long as you have a glass in your hand, people won't worry about its contents. You will be surprised to find that most people do not care about what you are drinking, they are more concerned about what *they* are drinking.
The people most likely to bother you about your choice of non-alcohol beverages are those with personality difficulties or drinking problems of their own. Deal with them firmly.

Relatives and friends

You will probably feel more at ease with yourself if you explain the true circumstances of your abstinence to close relatives and trusted friends. You will be pleasantly surprised, as the months pass, how they and the general public accept as an ordinary fact of life your new habit pattern as a non-drinker.

Alcohol and the home

There are divided opinions on whether or not to keep alcohol beverages in the home for other members of the family, friends and guests. Experience indicates that it may be unwise, and even unfair, to ask spouses, partners and close relatives to deny themselves on your account. It may lead to feelings of guilt on your part and feelings of resentment on theirs.

Safest and wisest

However, if you are living alone, or if your drinking career was focused around the home, particularly secret drinking, it is certainly safest and wisest to remove all alcoholic beverages for a certain period of time. You may prefer, as many people do, never to have alcohol in your home at all.

If your spouse, living partner, or other person in the home is a persistent heavy drinker and this is disturbing or interfering with your recovery, you may find it advisable to ask that person to leave the home on a temporary or permanent basis. Alternatively, you may find it necessary to leave home.

You are in charge

It is worth reminding yourself from time to time that you are a worthwhile, independent individual with your own priorities and your own goals in life. Do not be diverted from your positive course of action by your spouse, living partner, relatives, friends, or pressures from others.

Whatever you decide, it remains your sole responsibility to organize, with patience, your own recovery in the most effective ways to achieve success.

It is wise to read and re-read *Early days at ACCEPT* whilst you are attending the treatment programme.

Preliminary outcome data

To date, there have been no controlled trials comparing the PCCP model to traditional abstinence-based programmes. Two sets of preliminary outcome data have been gathered internally by ACCEPT (later ACCEPT/ARP), a voluntary sector day service which operated the PCCP model between November 1995 and March 1999. The model was altered during 1999 and the service was closed in June 2001.

The first set of figures compares early drop-out and abstinence rates before and after the PCCP model was established. The category 'Old model' refers to a standard full-time day programme of up to nine months attendance, offering a wide range of sessions consistent with the traditional psychosocial model.

	Old model	New model
	(78)	(46)
Failure to engage	23% (18)	14% (6)
(drop-out in first two weeks)		
Abstinence at 12 months	31% (24)	55% (25)

The second, larger set of data corresponds to all day client activity during a 30-month period between January 1996 and June 1998 (Elliott 2000):

- 132 clients join the day programme (maximum 24 at any one time).
- 17 fail to engage/drop out in first two weeks (13%).
- 115 remaining in the sample.
- 57 (50%) left in an unplanned manner at some time during their attendance on the day programme or Second Stage aftercare.[1]

---

[1] Drop-outs do not always relapse. In one study (Georgakis 1995), 16 per cent of drop-outs remained abstinent up to 30 months follow-up. Other drop-outs might have a further drinking episode and then abstain. Whether or not the treatment received prior to drop-out is a factor in these cases is difficult to determine.

- 58 (50%) left in a planned manner with attendance ranging from 8 to 30 weeks and a minimum of two weeks notice of leaving.
- Approximately 50% of clients who engaged with the day programme were known to be abstinent by direct weekly contact in Second Stage or by response to a questionnaire sent every 12 months.

References

Abraham K (1908) The psychological relations between sexuality and alcoholism. In (1979) Selected Papers on Psychoanalysis. New York: Brunner/Mazel.

Ainsworth MDS (1989) Attachments beyond infancy. American Psychologist 44(4): 709–16.

Alcohol Concern (1997) Statistics on Alcohol Consumption and Related Harm. Factsheet 4. London: Alcohol Concern.

Alcohol Concern (2000) Britain's Ruin. London: Alcohol Concern.

Alcohol Concern (2001) Alcohol and Crime. Factsheet 10. London: Alcohol Concern.

Alcohol Concern (2002a) Alcohol and Accidents. Factsheet 9. London: Alcohol Concern.

Alcohol Concern (2002b) Women and Alcohol – A Cause for Concern. Factsheet 2. London: Alcohol Concern.

Alcoholics Anonymous (1939) Alcoholics Anonymous. New York: AA World Services.

Alonso A, Rutan JS (1979) Women in group therapy. International Journal of Group Psychotherapy 29: 481–91.

American Psychiatric Association (1994) DSM-IV: Diagnostic and Statistical Manual of Mental Disorders, 4th edn. Washington, DC: APA.

Anthony JC, Warner L, Kessler R (1994). Comparative epidemiology of dependence on tobacco, alcohol, controlled substances and inhalants: basic findings from the National Comorbidity Survey. Experimental and Clinical Pharmacology 2(3): 244–68.

Arroyave F (1986) Some implications of transference and countertransference in the treatment of dependence. Journal of Analytical Psychology 31: 199–206.

Bateson G (1971) The cybernetics of self: a theory of alcoholism. Psychiatry 34(1): 1–18. Reprinted in Bateson G (1972), Steps to an Ecology of Mind. New York: Ballantine Books.

Beck AT, Wright FD, Newman CF, Liese BJ (1993) Cognitive Therapy of Substance Abuse. New York: Guilford.

Berg IK, Miller SD (1992) Working with the Problem Drinker: A Solution-focused Approach. New York: Norton.

Bien TH, Miller WR, Tonigan JS (1993) Brief interventions for alcohol problems: a review. Addiction 88: 315–36.

93

Bion WR (1962) The psychoanalytic study of thinking: a theory of thinking. International Journal of Psychoanalysis 43: 306–10.

Blazina C (2001) Analytic psychology and gender role conflict: the development of the fragile masculine self. Psychotherapy: Theory, Research, Practice, Training 38(1): 50–59.

Bott E (1987) The Kava ceremonial as a dream structure. In Douglas M (ed.), Constructive Drinking: Perspectives on Drink from Anthropology. Cambridge: Cambridge University Press. pp 182–204.

Bowlby J (1953) Some pathological processes set in train by early mother–child separation. Journal of Mental Science 99: 265–72.

Bowlby J (1969) Attachment and Loss, vol. I: Attachment. London: The Hogarth Press and The Institute of Psycho-Analysis.

British Medical Association (1989) Cited in Alcohol Concern (2001), Alcohol and Crime Statistics. London: Alcohol Concern.

Cameron D (1995) Liberating Solutions to Alcohol Problems: Treating Problem Drinkers Without Saying No. Northvale, NJ: Jason Aronson.

Cartwright A (1980) The attitudes of helping agents towards the alcoholic client: the influence of experience, support, training and self esteem. British Journal of Addiction 75: 413–31.

CASA (2002) Teen Tipplers: America's Underage Drinking Epidemic. New York: National Centre on Addiction and Substance Abuse at Columbia University.

Copello A, Godfrey C, Heather N et al. (2001) United Kingdom Alcohol Treatment Trial (UKATT): Hypothesis, design and methods. Alcohol and Alcoholism 36(1): 11–21.

Copello A, Orford J, Hodgson R, Tober G, Barrett C (2002) Social behaviour and network therapy: basic principles and early experiences. On behalf of the UKATT Research Team. Addictive Behaviours 27(3): 345–66.

Costello RM (1980) Alcoholism treatment effectiveness: slicing the outcome variance pie. In Edwards G, Grant M (eds), Alcoholism Treatment in Transition. Baltimore, MD: University Park Press.

DOH (1993) Health of the Nation Key Area Handbook: Mental Health. London: HMSO.

DOH (1999) Statistical Bulletin: Statistics on Alcohol 1976 Onwards. Bulletin 1999, 24. London.

DOH (2000) Smoking, Drinking and Drug Use Among Young People in England in 2000. London: The Stationery Office

Douglas M (ed.) (1987) Constructive Drinking: Perspectives on Drink From Anthropology. Cambridge: Cambridge University Press.

Drew LRH (1990) Facts we don't want to face. Drugs and Alcohol Review 9(3): 207–10.

Edwards G (2000) Alcohol: the Ambiguous Molecule. London: Penguin Books.

Edwards G, Gross MM (1976) Alcohol dependence: provisional description of a clinical syndrome. British Medical Journal 1: 1058–61.

Elliott B (1986) Gender identity in group analytic psychotherapy. Group Analysis 19(3): 195–206.

Elliott B (1987) Is unconscious really a dirty word? New Directions in the Study of Alcohol 13: 32–39.

Elliott B (2000) It's good to be jolted. Drug and Alcohol Findings 3: 22–23.

Emrick C (1975) A review of psychologically-oriented treatment of alcoholism II: the relative effectiveness of different treatment approaches and the effectiveness of treatment versus no treatment. Journal of Studies on Alcohol 36: 88–109.

Fenichel O (1945) The Psychoanalytic Theory of Neurosis. New York: W.W. Norton.

Flores PJ (1997) Group Psychotherapy with Addicted Populations: An Integration of Twelve-Step and Psychodynamic Theory, 2nd edition. New York: The Haworth Press.

Flores PJ (2001) Addiction as an attachment disorder: implications for group therapy. International Journal of Group Psychotherapy 51(1): 63–81.

Foster A (1979) The management of boundary crossing. In Hinshelwood RD, Manning N (eds), Therapeutic Communities: Reflections and Progress. London: Routledge and Kegan Paul.

Foulkes SH (1948) Introduction to Group-analytic Psychotherapy. London: Heinemann.

Foulkes SH (1964) Therapeutic Group Analysis. London: Allen and Unwin.

Freud S (1917) The development of the libido and the sexual organization. In Introductory Lectures on Psycho-Analysis, Lecture XXI, Part III, General Theory and the Neurosis. The Standard Edition of the Complete Psychological Works of Sigmund Freud. London: Hogarth Press.

Freud S (1920) Beyond the Pleasure Principle. The Standard Edition of the Complete Psychological Works of Sigmund Freud, vol. 18. London: Hogarth Press.

Freud S (1985) The Complete Letters of Sigmund Freud to Wilhelm Fliess. Translated and edited by JM Masson. Cambridge: Harvard University Press.

Galanter M (1993) Network therapy for substance abuse: a clinical trial. Psychotherapy 30: 251–58.

Georgakis A (1995) Clouds House: An Evaluation of a Residential Alcohol and Drug Dependency Treatment Centre. Commissioned by Anew Trust Ltd, Clouds House, East Knoyle, Salisbury, Wiltshire SP3 6BE.

Greenfeld LA (1998) Alcohol and Crime: An Analysis of National Data on the Prevalence of Alcohol Involvement in Crime. US Department of Justice, Office of Justice Programs, Bureau of Justice Statistics. Report no. NCJ-168632

HEA (1997) Alcohol. London: Health Education Authority.

HEA (1998) Perceptions of alcohol-related attendances in A and E departments in England: a national survey. Health Education Authority. Alcohol and Alcoholism 33(4): 354–61.

Heather N, Tebbutt J (eds) (1989) The Effectiveness of Treatment for Drug and Alcohol Problems. Monograph Series No. 11. Canberra: Australian Government Publishing Service.

Hester RK, Miller WR (eds) (1989) Handbook of Alcoholism Treatment Approaches: Effective Alternatives. Elmsford, NY: Pergamon Press.

Hinshelwood RD (1987) What Happens in Groups. London: Free Association Books.

Hopper E (1995) A psychoanalytical theory of 'drug addiction': unconscious fantasies of homosexuality, compulsions and masturbation within the context of traumatogenic processes. International Journal of Psycho-Analysis 76: 1121–42.

Horvath AO (1995) The therapeutic relationship: from transference to alliance. In Session: Psychotherapy in Practice, 1(1): 7–18.

Jackson M, Pines M, Stevens B (1986) Borderline personality: psychodynamics and treatment. Neurologia et Psychiatria 66–88.

Join Together (1998) Treatment for Addiction: Advancing the Common Good. Boston, Mass: Join Together.

Jones M (1956) The concept of the therapeutic community. American Journal of Psychiatry 112(8): 647–50.

Kennard D (1998a) Therapeutic communities are back and there's something a little different about them. Therapeutic Communities 19(4): 323–29.

Kennard D (1998b) An Introduction to Therapeutic Communities, 2nd edn. London: Jessica Kingsley.

Kernberg OF (1975) Borderline Conditions and Pathological Narcissism. New York: Jason Aronson.

Kernberg OF, Selzer MA, Koenigsberg HW, Carr AC, Appelbaum AH (1989) Psychodynamic Psychotherapy of Borderline Patients. New York: Basic Books.

Kessler RC, Nelson CB, McGonagle KA, Edmund MJ, Frank RG, Leap PJ (1996) The epidemiology of co-occurring addiction and mental disorders: implications for prevention and service utilization. American Journal of Orthopsychiatry 66(1): 17–31.

Khantzian EJ (1981) Some treatment implications of ego and self disturbances in alcoholism. In Bean-Bayog MH, Zinberg NE (eds), Dynamic Approaches to the Understanding and Treatment of Alcoholism. New York: The Free Press. pp 163–88. Reprinted in Khantzian EJ (1999) Treating Addiction as a Human Process. Northvale, NJ: Jason Aronson Inc. pp 85–116.

Khantzian EJ (1990) Self-regulation and self-medication factors in alcoholism and the addictions: similarities and differences. In Galanter M (ed.), Recent Developments in Alcoholism, vol. 8. New York: Plenum Press. pp 255–71. Reprinted in Khantzian EJ (1999) Treating Addiction as a Human Process. Northvale, NJ: Jason Aronson Inc. pp 181–202.

Khantzian EJ (1997) The self-medication hypothesis of substance use disorders: a reconsideration and recent applications. Harvard Review of Psychiatry 4: 231–44. Reprinted in Khantzian EJ (1999) Treating Addiction as a Human Process. Northvale, NJ: Jason Aronson Inc. pp 245–77.

Khantzian EJ (2001) Reflections on group treatments as corrective experiences for addictive vulnerability. International Journal of Group Psychotherapy 51(1): 11–20.

Khantzian EJ, Halliday KS, McAuliffe WE (1990) Addiction and the Vulnerable Self. New York: Guilford Press.

Kohut H (1977) The Restoration of the Self. New York: International University Press.

Krystal H (1982) Alexithymia and the effectiveness of psychoanalytic treatment. International Journal of Psychoanalytic Psychotherapy 9: 353–88.

Leighton T (1997) Borderline personality and substance abuse problems. In Ryle A (ed.), Cognitive Analytic Therapy and Borderline Personality Disorder: The Model and the Method. Chichester: Wiley.

Levin J (1987) Treatment of Alcoholism and the Addictions: A Self-Psychology Approach. New York: Jason Aronson.

Limentani A (1986) On the psychodynamics of drug dependence. Free Associations 5: 48–64.

Matano R, Yalom ID (1991) Approaches to chemical dependency: chemical dependency and interactive group therapy – a synthesis. International Journal of Group Psychotherapy 41(3): 269–94.

Mattson ME, Del Boca FK, Carroll KM et al. (1998) Compliance with treatment and follow-up protocols in Project MATCH: predictors and relationship to outcome. Alcoholism: Clinical and Experimental Research 22(6): 1328–39.

Mayfield D, McLeod G, Hall P (1974) The CAGE questionnaire: validation of a new alcohol screening instrument. American Journal of Psychiatry 131: 1121–23.

Meyers T, Smith J, Hancock G, Smith M (1999) Applying aspects of the community reinforcement approach to alcohol and drug services. Journal of Substance Use 4: 70–75.

Miller WR, Hester RK (1986) The effectiveness of alcoholism treatment: what research reveals. In Miller WR, Hester RK (eds), Treating Addictive Behaviour: Processes of Change. New York: Plenum Press. pp 121–74.

Miller WR, Brown JM, Simpson TL et al. (1995) What works? A methodological analysis of the alcohol treatment outcome literature. In Hester RK, Miller WR (eds) Handbook of Alcoholism Treatment Approaches: Effective Alternatives. Boston, Mass: Allyn and Bacon. pp 12–44.

Miller WR, Rollnick S (1991) Motivational Interviewing: Preparing People to Change Addictive Behaviour. New York: The Guilford Press.

Miller WR, Sanchez-Craig D (1996) How to have a high success rate in treatment: advice for evaluators of alcoholism programs. Addiction 91(6): 779–85.

Monahan C, Finney JW (1996) Explaining abstinence rates following treatment for alcohol abuse: a quantitive synthesis of patient, research design and treatment effects. Addiction 91(6): 787–805.

Moos R, Finney J, Cronkite R (1990) Alcoholism Treatment: Context, Process and Outcome. New York: Oxford University Press.

NHSDA (1996) National Household Survey on Drug Abuse: Main Findings. DHHS Publication No. (SMA) 98-3200. Bethesda, Md: United States Department of Health and Human Services.

NHTSA (1999) Traffic Safety Facts. National Center for Statistics and Analysis. Washington, DC: National Highway Traffic Safety Administration.

NIAAA (1998a) Alcohol and the Liver. Alcohol Alert 42, October 1998. Bethesda, Md: National Institute on Alcohol Abuse and Alcoholism.

NIAAA (1998b) Drinking in the United States: Main findings from the 1992 National Longitudinal Alcohol Epidemiologic Survey. NIH Publication No. 99-35198. Bethesda, Md: U.S. Department of Health and Human Services.

Ogden TH (1979) On projective identification. International Journal of Psychoanalysis 60: 357–73.

ONS (2000) Living in Britain: Results from the 1998 General Household Survey. Office for National Statistics. London: The Stationery Office.

OPCS (1994) The Prevalence of Psychiatric Morbidity Among Adults, 16–64, Living in Private Households in Great Britain. London: Office of Population Census and Surveys.

Orford J (1985) Excessive Appetites: A Psychological View of Addictions. Chichester: John Wiley and Sons.

Orford J, Edwards G (1977) Alcoholism: A Comparison of Treatment and Advice, with a Study of the Influence of Marriage. Oxford: Oxford University Press.

Pines M (1978) Group analytic psychotherapy and the borderline patient. Group Analysis 11(2): 115–26.

Pirmohamed M, Gilmore IT (2000) Alcohol abuse and the burden on the NHS – time for action. Journal of the Royal College of Physicians 34(2): 161–62.

Project MATCH Research Group (1993) Project MATCH: rationale and methods for a multisite clinical trial matching patients to alcoholism treatment. Alcoholism: Clinical and Experiential Research 17: 1130–45.

Rado S (1933) The psychoanalysis of pharmacothymia. Psychoanalytic Quarterly 2: 2–23.

Reading B (2002) The application of Bowlby's attachment theory to the psychotherapy of the addictions. In Weegmann M, Cohen R (eds), The Psychodynamics of Addiction. London: Whurr.

Robertson J (1958) Young Children in Hospital. London: Tavistock Publications.

Rodriguez de la Sierra L (2002) Countertransference: our difficulties in the treatment of substance abuse. In Weegman M, Cohen R (eds), The Psychodynamics of Addiction. London: Whurr. pp 141–52.

Roizen J (1997) Epidemiological issues in alcohol-related violence. In Galanter M (ed.), Recent Developments in Alcoholism, vol. 13. New York: Plenum Press. pp 7–40.

Roizen R, Cahalan D, Shanks P (1978) Spontaneous remission among untreated problem drinkers. In Kandel D (ed.), Longitudinal Research on Drug Use: Empirical Findings and Methodological Issues. Washington, DC: Hemisphere Press. pp 197–221.

Roller B, Nelson V (1999) Group psychotherapy treatment of borderline personalities. International Journal of Group Psychotherapy 49(3): 369–85.

Rosenfeld H (1960) On drug addiction. International Journal of Psycho-Analysis 41: 467–75.

Royal College of Physicians (1987) A Great and Growing Evil: The Medical Consequences of Alcohol Abuse. London: Tavistock.

Rychtarik RG, Prue DM, Rapp SR, King AC (1992) Self-efficacy, aftercare and relapse in a treatment programme for alcoholics. Journal of Studies on Alcohol 53(5): 435–40.

Rycroft C (1968) A Critical Dictionary of Psychoanalysis. London: Penguin Books.

Ryle A (1990) Cognitive Analytic Therapy: Active Participation in Change; A New Integration in Brief Psychotherapy. Chichester: John Wiley and Sons.

Saunders B, Allsop SJ (1991) Helping those that relapse. In Davidson R, Rollnick S, MacEwan I (eds), Counselling Problem Drinkers. London: Tavistock/ Routledge. pp 73–94.

Saunders W, Kershaw P (1979) Spontaneous remission from alcoholism – a community study. British Journal of Addiction 74: 251–66.

Selzer ML (1971) The Michigan Alcoholism Screening Test: the quest for a new diagnostic instrument. American Journal of Psychiatry 127(12): 1653–58.

Stevenson B, Ruscombe-King G (1993) Corking and uncorking: a reflection on group-analytic treatment for alcoholics. Group Analysis 26(3): 213–24.

UKATT Research Team (2001) United Kingdom Alcohol Treatment Trial (UKATT): hypotheses, design and methods. Alcohol and Alcoholism 36(1): 11–21.

USDHHS (2000) 10th Special Report to the US Congress on Alcohol and Health. United States Department of Health and Human Services. Bethesda, Md: National Institute of Health.

Vanicelli M (1982) Group psychotherapy with alcoholics: special techniques. Journal of Studies on Alcohol 41(1): 17–37.

Vanicelli M (1992) Removing the Roadblocks: Group Psychotherapy with Substance Abusers and Family Members. New York: The Guilford Press.

Vanicelli M (2001) Leader dilemmas and countertransference: considerations in group psychotherapy with substance abusers. International Journal of Group Psychotherapy 51(1): 43–62.

Velleman R (1992) Counselling Alcohol Problems. From Counselling in Practice Series (ed. Wendy Dryden). London: Sage Publications.

Walker RD, Donovan DM, Kivlahan DR, O'Leary MR (1983) Length of stay, neuropsychological performance, and aftercare: influences on alcohol treatment outcome. Journal of Consulting and Clinical Psychology 51: 900–911.

Wallace J (1978) Working with the preferred defense structure of the recovering alcoholic. In Zimberg S, Wallace J, Blume SB (eds), Practical Approaches to Alcoholism Psychotherapy. New York: Plenum Press. pp 19–29.

Washton AM (1992) Structured outpatient group therapy with alcohol and substance abusers. In Lowinson J, Ruiz P, Millman R (eds), Substance Abuse: A Comprehensive Textbook. Baltimore, Md: Williams and Wilkens.

Weegmann M (2002) The vulnerable self: Heinz Kohut and the addictions. In Weegmann M, Cohen R (eds), The Psychodynamics of Addiction. London: Whurr. pp 31–49.

Weldon EV (1994) Forensic psychotherapy. In Clarkson P, Porkorny MR (eds), The Handbook of Psychotherapy. London: Routledge.

Whiteley JS, Gordon J (1979) Group Approaches in Psychiatry. London: Routledge and Kegan Paul.

Winnicott DW (1953) Transitional objects and transitional phenomena. Reprinted in Winnicott DW (1971), Playing and Reality. London: Penguin Books.

Yalom ID (1975) The Theory and Practice of Group Psychotherapy, 2nd edn. New York: Basic Books, Inc.

Index